TH

Reveals the occult secrets of Odin's ancient magical alphabet, describing its pagan origins, history and divinatory use.

THE MAGIC OF THE RUNES
Their Origins and Occult Power

by

MICHAEL HOWARD

THE AQUARIAN PRESS
Wellingborough, Northamptonshire

First published 1980
Third Impression 1986

ISBN 0-85030-233-1 (UK)
ISBN 0-87728-467-9 (USA)

Printed in Great Britain by
Richard Clay (The Chaucer Press) Ltd,
Bungay, Suffolk

CONTENTS

CHAPTER ONE

ORIGINS OF THE RUNES

The Norse and Saxon runic alphabet is an ancient form of writing which is shrouded in historical and occult mystery. Very little is known of its magical uses although rune magic was widely practised for many hundreds of years. What scant information that is available has to be gleaned from obscure historical records, research into ancient religious practices, the surviving traditions of popular folklore and the weathered inscriptions on pagan and semi-Christian standing stones.

Definitions of the word rune are many and varied. It can be traced back to the Old Nordic and Anglo-Saxon *run*, early Icelandic *runar* and Old German *runa*. These in turn are derived from the Indo-European root word *ru*, which means alternatively 'mystery' or 'secret', and the Old High German *runer*, usually translated as 'whisper'. The slang term to rown, roon or round in the ear was widely used in Anglo-Saxon England to refer to the whispering of a secret and is obviously derived from rune.

From this popular usage (which is a good indication of sacred or taboo subjects transformed into common everyday situations) we can discern that the runes were a secret or semi-secret alphabet used by initiates of occult/pagan traditions to pass on magical information. They originated in the prehistoric rock carvings known as the Hallristinger script which were made by Neolithic and Bronze Age tribes who settled in Northern Italy. There is a distinct similarity between the runic alphabet and the old Etruscan forms of writing which seems to support the

theory of a North Italian origin. The unusual angular
strokes of the runes are probably due to the fact that they
were originally hewn into stone. Such actions would
prohibit the use of curves and rounded letters in the
alphabet. There is also a definite link between the runes and
the ancient Celtic alphabet of ogham and this will be
examined later in this book.

Odin – the God of the Runes

Mythologically, the invention of the runes is credited to the
Nordic god Odin. His name is said to be derived from the
Old Norse word *Od*, meaning wind or spirit. The Roman
historian and traveller Tacitus identified Odin or Woden
(as he was sometimes called by German pagans) with
Mercury, the Roman god who invented writing. The
physical description of Odin indicates his sinister
reputation. He is usually depicted as a tall, thin man
wearing a long cloak and with grey hair falling in tangled
locks to his shoulders. Odin's face is strong and hard, he has
only one eye which stares into the distance and burns blue.
His gaping eye socket is hidden by a wide-brimmed, soft hat
pulled down over one side of his face. He leans on a
blackthorn staff and is accompanied by a raven and a wolf.

Odin has the power to raise the dead, divine the future,
fly through the sky on his eight legged horse and change his
shape at will. Travellers would often meet the god as he
wandered the bleak winter landscape in human form. The
Danish king Harald Wartooth met him and the old god
promised the monarch immunity from wounds in battle. In
return King Harald pledged all the souls which his sword
drove from their bodies to Odin. However, when the king
betrayed Odin the god materialized at a battle in the shape
of his enemy and slew him. It seems that Odin cannot be
trusted to keep a pact.

Sometimes Odin is referred to by the name *Grim*. This is
an Old English term meaning 'hooded' or 'masked'. It
survives in the name Grimsdyke which is an ancient dyke at
Harrow Weald, Middlesex, obviously dedicated to the god.

Interestingly, the Celts possessed a divine hierarchy of hooded gods known as the Genii Cucullati or Hooded Ones. A stone plaque depicting three of these dieties was unearthed at Houseteads in Northumberland and dates from the third century c.e. (common era). Little is known of these gods except that they were associated with some kind of magical horse cult. This may be tenuously linked with the runes through the occult activities of the fraternity of Horse Whisperers who still survive in rural parts of East Anglia and the West Country. They claim to be able to tame wild horses by whispering magical incantations and seem to have originated in some pre-Christian religious cult which venerated the horse goddess. Although it is speculation, there may be a link here between Odin the hooded god, the Celtic Genii Cucullati and a pagan horse cult that used runes for magical purposes.

It is said that Odin gained his secret knowledge of the runes by a supreme act of self-sacrifice. He hung for nine days and nights impaled by his own spear to the Yggdrasill or World Tree to gain this forbidden wisdom. Nine is, of course, a lunar number representing the three phases of the moon (i.e. waxing, full and waning) multiplied by itself. In pagan mythology the moon is a symbol of inspiration, psychic power and the feminine aspect of Nature represented by the ever-fertile Earth Mother image. It is also said that Odin had drunk deeply from the sacred mead in the cauldron of inspiration, owned by the god Mimer, to learn the mysteries of life and death. The price he paid for this knowledge was the loss of an eye. The cauldron is an ancient symbol of the Great Mother Goddess and in these myths we can discern the relics of the old moon worship and earth magic which was slowly becoming subservient to the new patriarchy of the male gods.

The Secret of the Shamans

However we should not become too intoxicated by these fantastic tales of mighty gods and goddesses existing in some heavenly paradise beyond the North Pole. The possibility exists, and it is a strong one, that Odin may have been an historical personage who was deified after his death. This is a common theme in mythological history and some religious experts believe that the legends of such gods as Isis, Osiris, Bran and Bridget may be based on the lives of real people who civilized their respective countries and were worshipped as divine beings after they had passed on.

If this theory is tenable in the case of Odin then he may possibly have been a prehistoric shaman who discovered a magical alphabet after a ritual of self-sacrifice. Shamanism was the primitive (and I do not use the word in any derogatory way) religion of many parts of pre-Christian Europe and the shaman became a powerful figure in the tribal community and was both feared and respected. In anthropological terms the shaman is a man or woman with the psychic ability to contact the spirit world and communicate with its inhabitants. This was usually achieved while the shaman was in a trance-like state induced by drugs, ritual, dancing or fasting. The shaman also possessed the ability to divine the future, was able to find missing objects or persons by clairvoyant powers and could speak to the dead.

The shaman is 'different' from other people in a way which it is hard for we in the West, who have lost contact with the natural forces of our planet, to understand. Within his or her cultural situation the shaman is a unique person. They are feared because of their great powers for good and evil yet command the respect of those who depend on them. It is the shaman who protects the tribal community from its enemies (human or animal), ensures by magic a good harvest, knows the occult properties of herbs for healing the sick, can perceive the changing pattern of the future and, as his or her last gift to the dependent tribe, selects a replacement who will become the next shaman in line.

Shamanism still exists in many parts of the world and can be found in remote areas of Siberia (where even Communism has failed to destroy the old beliefs of the ethnic people who inhabit that icy region), in the East

Indies, North and South America, Africa and Australia.
Practitioners of the shamanistic tradition can even still be
found in the country districts of 'civilized' Europe where the
pagan religion survives under a thin veneer of token
Christianity. In all cases the shaman can be recognized by
his or her 'differentness' and the self-imposed isolation from
the community required in order to obtain the powers to
help it. The world of the shaman is so different from our
own that we would have to experience something of it before
we could fully understand its *modus operandi*. The shaman's
universe is completely magical. Nothing is simply ordinary,
nowhere are things exactly what they seem. His world has
no place for the single vision which the poet William Blake
said was the lack of imaginative response in Western
European culture. Everything has magical significance to
the shaman. He or she has learnt to read the signs and
omens placed by the Earth Mother in the natural world to
guide Her children and by gaining this knowledge can, in
turn, help those of us who lack this sublime vision of
creation.

Shamanistic Vision
It is almost impossible to convey the magical awareness
which the shaman possesses as a natural quality to
Westerners who have broken the umbilical cord to the
Earth Mother. In our times, matters of the spirit have either
been relegated to an occasional trip to the local Christian
church for a wedding, baptism or funeral or have become
the focus of outdated superstitions based on an irrational
fear of the unknown. We have wrapped ourselves up in a
technological cocoon and from its warm, cosy security make
two-fingered gestures of derision at the old, shamanistic
beliefs which were the origins of our present day religious
impulses. In fart' although the shaman may not be
'educated' in the way that the average person in the West
understands that word (i.e. conditioned from childhood to
accept a materialistic, single vision of the cosmic pattern)
his or her awareness of the natural environment in which we

live, breath, sleep and eventually die is a million times more concentrated and potent than the narrow image of the world which we experience through senses dulled and blurred by our unmagical civilization.

Just by walking down a woodland path, observing the texture and roundness of a stone, the colour of a dead leaf curled embryo-like on the earth, listening to the cries of the birds in the trees, feeling the elemental power of the wind or scrying the tracks of animals in the fresh snow, the shaman can tune in to the subtle vibrations of that state of being which exists in the nether regions between the worlds of matter and the realms of spirit. Such perception is a rare ability in our modern society but it is the treasured possession of a few rare individuals who understand and share the shamanistic view of life. These chosen few include among their ranks artists, poets, writers and mystics who can achieve the Oneness with the forces of Nature which is the mark of the true shaman and single him or her out from the rest of humanity.

Gateway to Occult Knowledge

How does the shaman gain this experience? There are various methods used to attain the special trance state which allows contact with the spiritual side of nature. These include the use by shamans of natural psychedelic agents such as the hallucination inducing 'sacred mushroom'. This is known by its Latin name as *amanita muscaria*. Other, safer methods of inducing trance are by breathing exercises, yoga techniques, sensory deprivation, fasting and ritual dance. There are also more hazardous methods such as flagellation, ritual sex and self-torture which were (and indeed still are) practised by the North American Indian shamans. If we return to the Norse legend of the hooded god Odin we find that he was impaled for nine days and nights by his own spear. At the end of this experience he achieved the vision of the magical runic alphabet. Similar rituals are known to the native Americans. Young braves are suspended by hooks dug deep into their flesh from the eaves of the medicine lodges. Pain is regarded by some priests of the native religions (rightly or wrongly) as a tool to open up the psychic centres of the body which, in Eastern mysticism, are termed the *chakras*.

Sacrificial Rites

In my previous book *The Runes and other Magical Alphabets* (Thorsons, Wellingborough) I mentioned the rites of initiation into the Odinic Mysteries. We speculated that these ceremonies included a symbolic sacrifice of the initiate by hanging him on a yew tree. Such a ritual gesture may have been a copy of the original act by which the god received the runic lore. At a later period this symbolic rite became debased and was interpreted in a more literal and horrific way as human sacrifice. This practice seems to have developed from the funeral rites of stabbing corpses with spears and then burning them, which was apparently an Odinist custom. However, a Christian abbot writing in the eleventh century c.e. gives a graphic description of the bodies of sacrificed men and animals hanging from trees around a temple to Odin at Uppsala in Sweden. Giving the good abbot the benefit of the doubt (Christian chroniclers of pagan rites were well known for their ability to distort the facts and exaggerate the 'nasty' aspects of the old beliefs, which they detested) it seems that such practices were performed at the temple at special festivals held every nine years to commemorate the death of the hooded god of the runes. Is it possible that the past appetite in this country for public hangings and the strong feelings at present flowing through the land to restore capital punishment may be an unconscious racial memory of these debased and cruel rites to Odin? In the world of magic anything is possible and the old *cliché* that truth is stranger than fiction is often perfectly correct.

Odin the Man

Support for the belief that Odin may have been a real person is offered by Robert Macoy. He claims that Odin

was originally the chieftain of an Asiatic tribe who
emigrated from his homeland, travelled across Central
Europe and settled finally in Scandinavia. There he
established a kingdom, formulated new laws and
established a mystery religion. He assumed the magical
name of Odin and founded a priesthood of twelve wise men
(representative of the zodiacal signs) who administered the
kingdom, celebrated the religious ceremonies and acted as
prophets, divining the future for the benefit of the local
people.

According to the American esoteric philosopher Manly
Palmer Hall, writing in his epic masterpiece *The Secret
Teachings of All Ages* (Philosophical Research Society[1]) this
historical Odin was mythologized after his death and
identified with a local god of the same name. This is a
similar process to the deification of the historical Jesus of
Nazareth, who, it would seem, was a Jewish rabbi with
extraordinary psychic powers. After his crucifixion he was
accepted by a minor group of Zionist extremists as the
Messiah promised by the Old Testament prophecies. In
pagan history, as we noted before, respected administrators
who acted as civilizers in periods of national stress were
often conferred with posthumous godships by their grateful
public. Today famous movie stars such as Rudolph
Valentino, James Dean and Marilyn Monroe have nearly
attained the same divine status in the eyes of their adoring
fans.

The Odinic Mysteries

Manly Palmer Hall states that the sacred mysteries of Odin
were celebrated in nine (again note the mystical lunar
number associated with the old moon worshippers) caves
which symbolically represented the nine ascending worlds
of spirit. The candidate for initiation into the Mysteries
symbolized Odin's son Baldur who was murdered by the

---

[1] U.K. distributors: Thorsons Publishers, Wellingborough,
Northants.

trickery of Loki, the Nordic personification of the powers of darkness, in an action-replay of the legend of the murder of the sun god Osiris by his brother/son Set in Ancient Egyptian mythology. Each cave that the initiate travelled through during the long and arduous ceremony also represented one of the spheres of nature. The priests who conducted the initiation ritual were symbols of the sun, the moon and the stars and also represented the planetary spirits associated with these heavenly bodies in northern myths.

The candidate eventually emerged from the last cave in the symbolic journey through the spirits worlds into a sacred inner sanctum that had a roof lined with battle shields. In this holy chamber the initiate took an oath of secrecy and a vow of allegiance to Odin. Finally, in recognition of the god, the initiate kissed the naked blade of a war sword. He then drank the special mead, laced with aromatic herbs, from a bowl made from a human skull. He was presented with a silver ring engraved with runic characters and told that he had passed through the gates of death and had been reborn as a perfected being.

If Manly Palmer Hall's account of the Odinic Mysteries can be accepted as fact, and there is little reason to doubt the authenticity of his research into ancient religious practices, the initiate not only represented Baldur but came face to face with an effigy of the god at the end of his journey through the nine worlds. This is a magico-religious practice which was well known in pagan initiatory rituals. In those involving a ceremonial maze when the neophyte reached the centre, he or she faced a bronze mirror reflecting back their own image. This was a way of teaching the initiate the meaning of the words engraved over the gate of the Delphic oracle 'Know Thyself' and also taught the lesson that the real spiritual truth cannot be found outside but must be experienced within.

Manly Hall states quite categorically that the burial mound of King Odin is said to be situated near the old god's major shrine at Uppsala in Sweden. We do not know if this folk legend has ever been verified by archaeological survey of the mound to see if a great chieftain is buried there. Despite this lack of verification it does provide further evidence that, in popular belief, Odin was an historical person who later became regarded as divine.

The Cult of Kingship

As Dr William Chaney states in his *Cult Of Kingship in Anglo-Saxon England* (Manchester University Press) almost every Anglo-Saxon Royal House claimed descent from their divine ancestor Woden or Odin. This allegiance to the old god – or rather his original, human representative, the ancient shaman priest-king – was brought to England by the invading Germanic tribes. Significantly, according to Dr Chaney, this belief survived the conversion of the Saxons to Christianity.

In Germanic and Scandinavian mythology and tribal society the king was the high priest of the Odinic Mysteries and was called, in Norse poetry, 'the warden of the holy temple of Odin'. In accordance with this belief the Royal Houses of the Anglo-Saxons were regarded as hereditary divine families descended from the high god Woden. It is therefore logical to assume that these rulers claimed lineal descent, either literally or symbolically, from the first tribal king who assumed the name Odin. He was the priest-king who received the sacred runic alphabet by means of a shamanistic rite of self-sacrifice.

Dr Chaney points out that the prefix 'Os', signifying 'heathen god' or 'divine', occurs in no less than twelve names of ancient Northumbrian kings. All but two of these died violently leading some folklore experts to suggest that they were sacrificial victims in the dark traditions of pagan Odinism. Dr Chaney regards the word 'Os' to be reminiscent of the spirits of the North Wind in Norse mythology and further states that it is a common term used by Icelanders to describe their pre-Christian dieties.

'Os' is also mentioned in a Saxon rune poem of the eighth or ninth century c.e. and is referred to as '... the beginning of every speech'. Dr Chaney says this refers to Odin who was the god that gave the magican words (i.e. the runes) that began every important statement or speech in Norse or Germanic tribal gatherings. Therefore we seem to have here a firm connection between the god Odin, the inventor of runes, the spirits of the North Wind, the Northumberland royal dynasty and the pagan belief in divine kingship.

Woden worship is said by Dr Chaney to have originated in the Rhineland or the south-east area of Europe. It was only later in history that the cult of the hooded rune god entered Northern Europe, carried by the migrating tribes of Indo-European peoples who were its devotees. This supports the theory of Robert Macoy who postulates an Asian warrior king who, migrating northwards from his tribal homelands, established a divine kingdom in Scandinavia, based on sacrificial ceremonies, magical alphabets and shamanism.

CHAPTER TWO

RUNIC SCRIPTS

There were, and indeed are, many different types of runic alphabets and letters. Probably the most common is the Germanic *fuþark* (the 'þ' is pronounced as 'th'). This runic alphabet consists of twenty-four runes divided up into three groups of eight which were called Freyja's Eight, Hagal's Eight and Tiw's Eight. The entire sequence of these runic letters has so far only been found on a fifth century c.e. standing stone in Kylver, Sweden.

The Germanic *fuþark* runes remained popular until the late eight century c.e. when, probably with the invasion of the Norsemen, Scandinavian forms of runes were imported into Britain. These new alphabets were characterized by having either fourteen or sixteen runes. However, by the ninth century c.e., in parts of northern England, alphabets of up to thirty-three runes were in use for magical, legal and religious purposes.

Viking and Danish raids on the eastern countries of England and the eventual occupation of large tracts of land by the foreign invaders increased the influence of Scandinavian runes during the eighth and ninth centuries. One of the most famous of the Norse runic inscriptions can be seen on an eleventh century c.e. stone discovered in St Pauls' churchyard in London. It now stands in the Guildhall museum and bears the inscription 'Finna and Roki had me set up'. Runic inscriptions found on crosses and standing stones in the Isle of Man are occasionally interspersed with the Old Celtic ogham writing. This provides a strong connection between these two magical alphabets which we will be returning to later.

Different varieties of runes and their use, either together or intermixed, make it extremely difficult for students of the alphabet to trace back its origins properly. We find Germanic runes, Old English or Saxon runes, Scandinavian (Norwegian, Swedish and Danish) runes and Gothic runes. During the romantic revival of the eighteenth century – when rich aristocrats dabbled in the occult, built fantastic follies and joined such orgiastic organizations as the Hellfire Club – psuedo-runes became popular. Some inscriptions featuring these phoney runic alphabets may still survive and add one more headache to the investigator seeking reliable information on this historical enigma.

The Symbolic Meaning of the Rune Scripts

In my previous book I rationalized the various runic alphabets into a variant of the Germanic *fuṗark*. For the purpose of this book, so as not to confuse the reader, we will stay with this version. The alphabet is as follows.

F U TH A R K W N I

P Z S B M L D O

The development of these runes into the orthodox Latin alphabet which we are all taught at school can be seen by the similarity between some of the runic characters and the letters we use today. Although the runes had their equivalents in the Latin letters for writing purposes, their real magical significance and power came from the symbolic meanings attributed to each of them by the Rune magicians. A version of these magical meanings is given below. In each case the Old English word for each rune is also given.

Feoh. Cattle. These were a form of currency in

olden times and were used instead of money in transactions.

ᛒ   *Beorc*. Birch twig. This is a reference to the fertility rites of the pagan Old Religion. In folklore a beating with birch twigs had both a sexual and magical significance and was said to be lucky. This was a folk memory of ritual flagellation during fertility ceremonies. In the rituals of the pagan ways the altar was sometimes the naked body of a priestess. Traditionally she would lie on a bed of birch twigs and wild flowers.

ᚦ   *Porn*. In the original Germanic language the name of this rune referred to a giant or demon. However in the Old English tongue it translates as *thorn*. Early magicians or shamans used a wand or staff made of blackthorn. Such magical weapons possessed the power to curse and could blast the souls of the magus' enemies. In such cursing spells the shaman would evoke the ice giants of Norse mythology or even the mighty thunder god Thor who wielded a thunderbolt of elemental power. This rune could also be used to evoke and control the demons which the old Norse folk believed haunted the dark forests and grey lakes of their homeland.

ᚩ   *Os*. This was the rune of the gods and Odin in particular. It granted the user the gift of communication with the divine realms. Used in its singular form the rune magician could contact Odin directly.

ᚱ   *Rad*. This rune signifies a long journey on horseback. In spiritual symbolism it relates to the last journey undertaken by the soul from the body to Valhalla, the afterworld fit for heroes.

ᚲ   *Ken*. A torch or symbol of the pre-Christian cults of sun worship. Bonfires were lit on the high hills at the solstices and equinoxes to mark the progression of the sun across the sky in pagan times. These dates were the Winter and Summer Solstices (December 22nd and June 21st), which were the shortest and longest days respectively, and the Spring and Autumn Equinoxes (March 21st and September 22nd), when the hours of the day equal the hours of the night. The solstices and equinoxes also marked

the transition points of the four fixed signs of the Zodiac,
which are: Capricorn the Goat (Winter Solstice); Aries
(Spring Equinox); Cancer the Crab (Summer Solstice);
and Libra the Scales (Autumn Equinox).

Sun worship was widespread in pagan Scandinavia and
was associated with a male priesthood. Interestingly
enough *Ken* is sometimes spelt *Kano* which is a word used in
connection with the fertility goddess Nerthus. As we know
the male-dominated solar worship replaced, to some extent
the older, lunar fertility cult of the Great Mother which was
widespread in Stone Age Europe. The different spelling
and meaning of this rune, and its symbolism, could indicate
just how old runic writing really is, for ritual seasonal fires
were also a feature of the ancient religion of the Goddess.

✕ *Gyfu* means simply 'a gift offered to the gods'. This
is a polite pagan euphemism for sacrifice, which could
either be an animal or, at its most debased, a human being.
This is an aspect of pagan religions which it is difficult to
defend. However we have no real reason to be smug about
such grisly activities when we still have the ritual slaughter
of the abattoir and the obscene horrors of vivisection. In
modern terms war can also be regarded as a form of human
sacrifice although, judging from the twentieth century, the
god of war has an insatiable appetite for blood.

In the ceremonies to Odin, criminals found guilty of
capital offences or captured prisoners-of-war were sentenced
to ritual death. The usual weapon of execution was a
leather thong to strangle the victim. We can therefore be
sure that the act was performed quickly and death was
relatively painless. This method of ritual strangulation is an
ancient practice predating the Viking Iron Age. Examples
of the practice are to be found in Bronze Age burials in the
peat bogs of Denmark. There mummified bodies have been
found with leather or willow nooses around their necks.
According to Professor P.V. Glob of the Danish National
Museum, author of *The Bog People*, the unearthed bodies
were sacrificial victims dedicated to the Great Mother
Goddess. In India similar practices existed in the days of

the British Raj when the cult of Thuggee created terror by
assassinating leading members of the community with
leather nooses. This bizarre form of ritual murder earned
the Thuggee cultists the nickname The Stranglers and it
was said that they dedicated the souls of their victims to the
dark Hindu goddess Kali.

In 1891, a huge silver cauldron was excavated at
Gundestrup in Denmark. It had engraved on its sides
representations of gods and goddesses, fantastic animals
and a bloodchilling sacrificial scene. In this a large figure
(who is possibly a high priest) is in the process of lowering a
smaller figure (probably a child) head first into a ritual
container or cauldron. The Greek traveller Strabo described
such a practice among the Germanic tribes.

> Among the women who accompanied them on their war-like
> expedition were prophetesses who were also priestesses. They
> were grey with age and wore white clothes and over them
> cloaks of the finest linen with metal belts. They were also
> barefoot. These women entered the camp, swords in hands,
> went up to the prisoners [of war] and led them to a bronze
> vessel which held some twenty measures. One of the women
> would mount the step and, leaning over the container, cut the
> throat of the prisoner who was held over the vessel's rim.

If the sacrificial victim was not a felon or a prisoner from
another tribe it was not unusual for the king or chieftain to
volunteer to die for his tribe. He became the human
representative of the god and his blood was believed to
possess the magic power to fertilize the earth and bring a
good harvest. Such old pagan beliefs die hard. It is factually
recorded than when King Charles I was beheaded the
crowd pressed forward with handkerchiefs to mop up the
spilt blood. These bloodsoaked cloths were credited later
with the miraculous power to heal the sick and bring good
fortune to their owners.

▽ *Wyn* meant joy or glory. An odd tale about Odin
may be connected with the meaning of this rune. It is
recorded that the one-eyed god of wisdom took 'nine glory

twigs and smote an adder so it fell in nine pieces'. These glory twigs are obviously rune staves of some kind and may have been carved with this particular rune hence their name.

Haegl was snow, hail and ice which was ever present in the cold climate of the North Lands. It was also the natural weapon of the frost giants and the ice demons who lurked in the winter blizzard to strike down unwary travellers.

Nyd was the need or necessity which drives men and women on to accomplish impossible deeds. In the time of the Saxons and the Vikings survival was a hard struggle. Myriad dangers had to be faced every day to survive and included, famine, pestilence, attacks by wild animals and raids by other tribes. This rune was also the special one associated with a person's fate or destiny and, in a divinatory sense, this rune represents troubles in the path of life from which lessons can be learnt.

Ger. A spear. The prime weapon of both Odin and the god of war, Tiw (who gave his name to our Tuesday). Spears were also carried into battle by every Saxon and Norse warrior. In runic texts from Russia we read of spear heads engraved with runes which read 'attacker' and 'weapon that makes the enemy run away'. Both these runic inscriptions were found surrounded by magical sigils such as the solar disc, the crescent moon, the swastika and the triskele or life force symbol. Spears were also used in human sacrifice as we shall see later in this book.

Eoh. Yew. A tree sacred to runecraft for its wood was often carved into rune wands or staves. These staves often became runic calendars known as 'primstaves' or 'golden numbers'. Those specifically from Scandinavia were called 'rimstocks' from 'rim' meaning calendar and 'stock' meaning stick. It is reported that such devices were still used in rural country districts in Sweden as late as the nineteenth century.

They were in various shapes and sizes. Sword-shaped or plain straight, varying in length from a few inches to several feet, made as walking sticks, oval rings or square tablets of wood or bone. The days of the year were shown in runic characters with the feasts and religious dates signified by symbols which were often in animal form. The nineteen 'golden numbers' for calculating the phases of the moon were also included.

These calendars are of pagan origin but the earliest examples so far discovered date only from the early medieval period. This fact offers us proof of the survival of pagan beliefs in Scandinavia after the alleged conversion of the country to the new Christian religion.

Incidentally, in English folklore the yew tree was superstititously regarded by country people as the tree of the dead. It is to be found in profusion planted in old country churchyards where it is said to have the power to protect the dead and prevent them haunting the living.

ᛈ *Pear* is one of the mystery letters in the runic alphabet and to date has eluded translation by Anglo-Saxon and Norse scholars. Several rather far-fetched explanations of its meaning have been put forward by some occultists but none is convincing enough to mention here.

ᛉ *Eolh.* Defence or protection. A magical rune to keep away trespassers on private property or to generally protect the user from harm. Such runes were frequently carved on the lintels over burial mounds or on standing stones underneath which were concealed the cremated ashes of important priests or tribal leaders. The runic sigil itself may be derived from their ritual gesture of the splayed hand or the two horned sign used to ward off the evil eye.

ᛋ *Sigel* means, quite literally, the sun which, as we have said earlier, was an important object of worship in the Bronze Age and Iron Age cultures. In prehistoric rock carvings the sun is often symbolized by the magical sign of the swastika. This is probably the most misunderstood of all pagan symbols and, because of its association in the popular mind with fascism, is seldom worn in public by modern followers of the Old Religion.

Unfortunately, the swastika was accepted by the German

National Socialist (Nazi) Party as their logo and since the last war has been tainted with the horrors of their crimes. In fact, it is one of the oldest magical symbols known to humanity and is widely found all over the world in prehistoric cave art where it represents the sun and the whirling energy of the Life Force. Other forms of it are the sun wheel of the Navajo; the spiral of the Hopi Indians in North America; the Celtic equal-armed cross which was adopted by the early Christians; and the three-footed national badge of the Isle of Man.

It is a very potent symbol and, in the ancient Hindu language Sanskrit, it is known as 'All is Well' and in Anglo-Saxon is called the flyfot, or 'many footed', cross. Swastikas have been found in Persia, Greece, India, Scandinavia, France, Mexico, Yucatan, Finland and South America. Its shape denotes the passage of the sun across the heaven and so powerful is the swastika that it is regarded in pagan belief as the symbol of both the Earth Mother and the Sky Thunder God.

↑   *Tyr* or *Tiw* was the Norse god of war. Runes shaped like this were carried by the Vikings on their shields when they went into battle, engraved on the hilts or blades of their swords or worn on special amulets around the neck. Any warrior who openly wore the sign of Tiw as he went into battle was believed to become possessed of incredible strength and courage. The Vikings believed that no mortal man could stand up to a person protected by the magical power of this rune.

The Odinist religion, of course, had an elite class of warrior priests who were called *berserkers*. This name comes from the Norse meaning 'bear shirt' or 'wolf skin' and seems to refer to the shaggy pelts worn by Viking warriors when they went into battle against their enemies.

These *berserkers* were fanatical in their loyalty to Odin and Tiw and wore swords richly decorated with runes. From descriptions of these weapons their superstitious enemies may have concocted tales of magical swords which thirsted for blood and were invincible.

The *berserkers* were naked under their animal skins and were credited with the power to shape-shift into bears or wolves by the recitation of certain secret runes. Such an idea may have originated in the speed and dexterity of the Vikings to doff and don their animal tunics and their bloodcurling war chants which resembled the howls and growls of wild animals.

$\bowtie$ *Mannaz*. Man. This rune refers to the human race or to an individual member of the tribe. In divination it sometimes represents the enquirer and can only be properly interpreted by consulting the runes near it in the reading.

$\restriction$ *Lagu* or *Laguz*. Water. This rune signifies the sacred liquid in the womb of the Great Mother Goddess from where, according to pagan belief, the human race originated.

$\gtrless$ *Ing* meant 'the Danes', who were one of the principal Scandinavian peoples to use the runes for both magical and secular purposes.

$\Diamond$ *Odal* represents inherited land or property.

$\bowtie$ *Dueg* was the day when the Sun was at its most powerful. As rune magic was deeply rooted in pagan solar religion of the northern and Saxon tribes, this day was an important one on their calendars.

Individual runic letters and combinations of letters were grouped together to form magical incantations for cursing, healing and predicting by the Rune Masters who were a powerful spiritual caste in pagan tribal society as we shall see next.

CHAPTER THREE

THE RUNE MASTERS

Before examining the magical qualities of the runic alphabet it would be prudent to discover a little more about the people who used the runes and especially about those chosen few who claimed to be adepts in ancient rune magic.

The wizards who used the runes for magical purposes regarded themselves as blood kin to Odin, the Nordic god who was popularly accredited with inventing the runic alphabet. As we have seen, they were basically followers of the shamanistic tradition which is one of the oldest, if not the oldest, religious belief system known to humanity. Beliefs which dated back to the early Stone Age people and their simplistic, yet essential, concept of the Life Force which they symbolized in art and ritual as a male Horned God and a female Moon Goddess or Earth Mother.

According to the Scottish occultist and writer Lewis Spence the term 'shaman' is derived from a Manchurian word meaning 'one who is excited'. This is a direct reference to the state of near hysteria cultivated by the shaman in order to communicate with the spirits of the departed and the elemental inhabitants of the mystical Otherworld that exists beyond the material senses. A shaman can, in theory, be of any religion yet is of none for he or she (the term is a neutral one without gender, like witch) is a disciple of the oldest religion practised by humanity.

Shamanistic Training
Shamanism, like hereditary witchcraft, is passed down in families from generation to generation. It is usually

transmitted from mother to daughter and father to son. When a person decides to take up the shaman's cloak he or she retires into the forest or tundra for three days to prepare for the traumatic experience of initiation. During this period the shaman lives in harmony with nature and refuses to partake of food or drink. During this period of enforced isolation the novice receives his or her mediumistic powers (the ability to speak with spirits) through the magical action of some natural object. This object may be a stone, a tree or an animal which becomes a ritual totem or power source for the shaman when he or she returns to the tribe.

The psychic training of a shaman lasts for two to three years at the minimum. It consists of occult exercises designed to open up the psychic centres in the body and allow contact with the guardian spirits of the Otherworld. Physical training, which is just as arduous as the controlling of the psychic side of the shaman's abilities, consists of instructions by the elders of the tribe in the ritual and seasonal dances, magical songs and the use of the special spirit drum which is used by the shaman to make contact with the underworld.

The spirit drum was the most important magical instrument used in the shamanistic ceremonies. It was similar to the traditional Irish or Scottish bodhrann drum which today is a feature of many folk music groups. It is very basically constructed from a wooden hoop over which is stretched tight animal hide or a piece of velum. This is fixed in place by brass tacks to form a completely rigid playing surface. No iron can be used in the construction of this drum for it is an old belief that this metal negates the power raised in magical rites. Shamanistic spirit drums had occult symbols or demon faces painted on their surfaces and runic characters etched around the rim. The drum could be played either with the flat of the hand or by using a double-headed drumstick carved from wood or bone.

Shamans often received instructions and occult teachings through dreams which in many cases were like visions. In these dreams the spirits of the Otherworld materialized in

the shape of animals and spoke to them. Such experiences
are a common feature of magical initiation especially in
ethnic societies. Recently, psychologists such as Dr Carl
Jung have carefully researched the hidden symbolism of
dreams and have discovered that they are an important
aspect of personal development. Whether we remember
them or not every person dreams and those which are in
colour or spring easily to our conscious mind when we
awake are important and should be analysed carefully. In
dreams the subconscious yields its many secrets and we can
contact the archetypal images which lurk in the racial
memory of all of us. We can indeed become our own
shamans.

Shamanistic Initiation

An important part of the shamanistic initiation rituals was
the ceremony known as the 'Ascent of the Tree'. This
involved the setting up of a birch pole in a forest clearing. A
goat or some other small animal was sacrificed and its blood
smeared on the nine openings of the shaman's naked body
to seal them from invasion by negative forces. The master
shaman then climbed the pole, cutting nine notches in it as
he went. The initiate then followed the master shaman up
the birch pole in a journey which was symbolic of the soul's
ascension through the nine worlds of heaven. The birch pole
used in this ceremony represents the pillar or sacred tree
which stands at the centre of the world and points up at the
North Star which is the realm of the old gods. This sacred
tree connects the material world of the senses with the
spiritual sphere of the psyche. When the shaman listens to
the hypnotic beat of the spirit drum he astrally projects his
soul to the World Tree (the Yggdrasill in Norse mythology)
which is the ladder of ascension to the spirit kingdom.

As soon as the shaman has passed all the tests set by his
master and completed his psychic and physical training a
special ceremony takes place during which the new recruit
is formally accepted as a full-blooded wizard. He is led to
the top of a hill dressed in ceremonial regalia which will

include the pelts of several sacred animals. He is handed a
magic rattle and told to repeat a vow of fidelity to the
matters of the spirit and renounces all wordly things. The
final initiation of the new shaman comes when he is given
his familiar spirits who will remain with him until his death,
when they vanish. A similar tradition is recorded in the
accounts of traditional witches in rural England.

Often the initiation rituals include, as do so many pagan
rituals, a symbolic act of death and rebirth. In the
ceremonies of certain Eskimo shamans the neophyte
remains for many hours meditating in an igloo. After a
period of time has lapsed he becomes unconscious and
remains in a state of coma for three days. During this self-
imposed trance he experiences intense visions which include
meetings with shadowy demons from the underworld and
being eaten alive by a giant polar bear. Eventually the
shaman regains consciousness and, in the terminology of
psycho-magical experience, is reborn as a new personality.
While in the trance he has been cleansed of his past errors
and defects in character and emerges from the icy womb of
the igloo as an enlightened being.

Among the tribal communities of northern Siberia,
Finland and Lapland the shaman combined the role of
medicine man, priest and prophet. He was also the medium
used by the tribe to make contact with the spirits of the
dead and predict the future. In the case of the latter he may
well have used the runes for divination. Alternatively, he
would have employed the spirit drum, using its steady beat
to fall into a trance during which prophecies would be
uttered and advice given. Sometimes the shaman spoke in
strange languages or unknown dialects. Often he would
become possessed by spirits and some of these would try to
bring harm to the shaman and those gathered around his
entranced body.

The Regalia of the Rune Masters
Shamans were the spiritual descendants of the sorcerers
and priest-magicians of the Stone and Bronze Ages. Some of

the remains of these practitioners of the occult arts have been discovered, almost perfectly preserved, in the peat bogs of Denmark. One of these burials was unearthed at Lyngby near Copenhagen at the end of the nineteenth century. Archaeologists excavating the site discovered the remains of an oak coffin which contained the skeleton of a man who had obviously been a shaman.

In the coffin was a leather bag containing amber heads (which in neolithic times had a magical significance which survives to this day in folklore), a conch shell (a fertility symbol which was a thinly disguised representation of the female sexual organs), a falcon's claw (possibly a hunting amulet or magic charm granting the power to fly), the bones of a snake (traditionally associated with healing), a squirrel's tail and the dried entrails of a small rodent.

The archaeologists who examined this find believed they had stumbled on the burial place of a local priest-magician. Confirmation came when they found a forked hazel twig in the coffin wrapped in animal skin. This they identified as a magical wand or sceptre of office carried by the ancient shaman as a token of his power.

In fact the shamans and rune masters of Northern Europe were easily distinguished from ordinary people by their distinctive regalia which denoted their special calling. They wore ritual head dresses made from the fur of woodland creatures such as the badger and the fox, a woollen cloak, dyed blue – one of the sacred colours of the Norse god Odin – and carried a leather pouch filled with dried herbs and charms. As a mark of their trade the rune masters carried a special staff or baton made of ash or hazel wood which was carved with runic sigils.

Unusual costumes worn by high-ranking initiates were also known in the annals of European witchcraft which was a debased form of the old animistic religion followed by the shaman priests. A seventeenth century portrait of a male witch, described by witchdraft writer Dr Margaret Murray in one of her articles for the journal of the Folklore Society, provides us with an eye-witness description which supports this notion. The portrait depicts a moon-faced man clad in a faery-green hood with bells like a jester's cap and a russet-coloured jerkin. He holds in his strong hands a brindle cat which is obviously supposed to be his familiar.

Writing in 1584 Reginald Scot, author of *The Discoverie of Witchcraft*, mentioned a kind of uniform worn by prominent witches. Such magical attire seems to have survived even today. In 1946 it was reliably reported that East Anglian witches possessed a ceremonial costume which was passed down from generation to generation. It consisted of three weasel, stoat or polecat skins worn around the neck and hanging down between the breasts like a kind of ritual collar. Special decorations of this type were apparently sported by Suffolk witches in the pre-war years.

In *The Saga of Erik the Red* an anonymous author writing in the late thirteenth century c.e. provides us with an interesting description of a Rune Mistress.

> She wore a cloak set with stones along the hem. Around her neck and covering her head [was] a hood of white catskin. In one hand she carried a staff with a knob at the end. At her belt, holding her dress together, was a charm pouch. She wore catskin shoes and mittens to cover her hands.

An Icelandic seeress and runecaster describes her magical talents in the following folk song.

> Hedi, me call me when their homes I visit.
> A far seeing witch, wise in talismans,
> Caster of spells, cunning in magic,
> To wicked women welcome always.
>
> Arm rings and necklaces Odin ye gave me,
> To learn my lore, to learn all magics,
> Wider and wider, through all worlds I see.
>
> Outside I sat myself when ye came,
> Terror of the gods and gazed in my eyes,
> What do ye ask of me?
> Why tempt me?

Odin! O know ye, I know where thy lost eye has gone,
Hidden deep in Mimir's well,
Mimir each man's mead he drinks,
Well, would ye know more.

The reference in the second verse to the arm rings and
necklaces given to the witch by the hooded god may refer to
magical bracelets and pendants which were marks of her
status in the tribe. In the third verse, first line she refers to
astral travel. This is the occult technique of projecting the
spirit from the physical body at will. It was a skill practised
by the northern shamans and the secret knowledge of its
practice was inherited by later rune masters and mistresses.

Runic Skill

Incorrect use of a rune could spell deadly danger for the
magician or witch. The old Rune Masters believed that
every rune was associated with an elemental spirit or force
which had to be carefully evoked and once conjured into
physical form had to be very carefully controlled. If this
entity escaped the magician then it would be unleashed on
an unsuspecting world and create havoc. Some of the spirits
evoked by the shamans were believed by them to be succubi
and incubi. These were lustful earth spirits who delighted in
sexual relations with humans in the shape of beautiful
women or handsome young boys. Their carnal appetites
were insatiable and any person who became possessed by
them could be literally fornicated to death.

There was also the real danger that people who had not
received the proper occult training in runecraft could
dabble with them and both hurt themselves and others. For
instance, the use of a cursing rune when a healing one was
required would have dire results for both the patient and
the would-be rune master who would have to face the
vengeance of the victim's relatives.

One famous Rune Master named Egill was called to a
house where a woman laying dying from a fever. A rival
Rune Master had already been called in to minister to the
sick woman but despite his assistance she hovered on the

brink of death. Egill immediately identified the source of the trouble. His rival had scored the wrong runes on a fragment of whale bone hanging above the patient's bed. Angrily, Egill denounced the quack runecasters who claimed to be skilled in runic magic yet lacked the knowledge to apply runic lore correctly.

> Runes shall not a man score,
> save he can read them well,
> that many a man betideth on a
> mirk stave to stumble,
> saw I on a scraped whale bone
> ten dark staves scored
> thou hath to the leek widen
> over long sickness broughton.

The skilled rune master immediately erased the incorrect runes on the bone and replaced them with his own runic healing charm. This he placed under the sick woman's pillow and within a few minutes she was restored to full health once more.

Egill was very well versed in the secrets of the runes. Once he narrowly escaped death at the hands of an assassin, hired by a rival magician, by using the runes. He carved runes around the rim of a drinking cup which he suspected had been poisoned by his enemy. These he reddened with his own blood and immediately the drinking horn shattered into fragments and its tainted contents were spilt on the floor. If the drink had not been poisoned the runes would not have broken the cup.

CHAPTER FOUR

USES OF THE RUNES

How did the ancient rune masters believe the runes worked? As there are no written records concerning runic magic (like most genuine occult knowledge the secrets of the runic alphabet were passed from person to person by word of mouth only) it is very difficult to find out why the Norse and Saxon people had such a strong belief in the potency of these strange mystical letters. They certainly regarded the runes as a special alphabet to be used only for magical purposes, healing, cursing and the wording of legal contracts or pacts between tribes or individuals which could never be broken.

We referred earlier to the elemental spirits associated with the runes which were regarded as the major source of their mysterious power. In some cases these entities are the gods and goddesses of the Old Norse religion. As runecraft faded under the baleful influence of the Christian Church and its black-robed priests, the once mighty gods of the North degenerated into lesser spirits, faeries or demons. There is an old saying which is very true that the gods of the old religion become the devils of the new one and the debasement of the pagan dieties by Christianity is a prime example of this in action.

Nordic Gods
The gods of the Nordic pantheon were a larger than life, lusty crowd who seemed to have spent their time fighting, eating and drinking or indulging in orgiastic merry-making. They were therefore perfect reflections of the people who worshipped them. Originally, of course, the Stone Age

people believed only in the Life Force represented by a god
or goddess known as the Lord and Lady. As human
religious concepts became more sophisticated the divine
couple became a whole pantheon of gods and goddesses
who symbolized a different aspect of the one Creative
Principle which brought the universe into existence.

Thor

Scandinavian mythology had many gods, like so many
other pagan religions, and each one had characteristics
which were connected with the esoteric meanings of the
runes. There was Thor who was a typical Indo-European
thunder sky god. His magical weapon was a huge hammer
or thunderbolt which he used to destroy his enemies and kill
the ice giants which haunted the north lands. He was
invoked in rune magic as an avenging force and was popular
with rune magicians skilled in curses. In Ireland an old
name for the Vikings was 'the People of Thor' because of
their courage in battle and bloodthirsty fighting habits.

Frigg

Frigg was a goddess of fertility and was possibly a Nordic
version of the Earth Mother. She has lent her name to a
slang word for female sexual activity which suggests that
she may be connected with the ritual marriage held in the
spring to encourage the crops to grow. She is associated by
some experts in Nordic religion with a later version of the
Bronze Age fertility goddess Nerthus. This deity was
represented at ceremonies by a naked priestess with long
hair wearing a torc (gold necklace) and arm and leg
bracelets who rode in a sacred wagon.

Freyja

A second important goddess in the Norse pantheon was
Freyja who is connected with an elite sisterhood of priestesses known as the *volva* who were renowned for their prophetic utterances. These women seem to have been female
shamans and were consulted by the tribe on important

matters such as if the harvest was going to be a good one or whether sickness would come to the land. They allegedly possessed the power granted to them by Freyja of shape-shifting into bird form and travelling over the countryside, but this sounds as if it is a garbled description of astral travel. The *volva* had familiar spirits in the shape of cats (shades of the medieval witch trials) and it is recorded that Freyja used to ride across the sky in a chariot drawn by black cats.

Baldur

Of the male gods, Baldur was the youngest and the most beautiful. He was the god of summer and the sun and it is said his face shone like gold, his hair was like fine gold and his eyes glowed radiant blue. His mother was Frigg, goddess of the fertile earth, and he was the son of the mighty Odin. His father had engraved his tongue with speech runes so that he was the most eloquent speaker among all the Norse gods.

Unfortunately Baldur's popularity and good looks were resented by the Fire god Loki who plotted the downfall of the beautiful young god. Baldur fell ill and it seemed as if nothing could save him from a lingering death. His father chanted runes over his inert body but the god slowly sank to the lowest ebb of consciousness, complaining of strange dreams which disturbed his mind. Frigg made all living things under her protection as Mother of the Earth to swear an oath that they would not harm Baldur. She even made the plants, stones and metals swear this sacred oath. The only plant that did not make the promise was the mistletoe. Frigg asked no vow of it because it had no power of its own and clung to the oak tree for protection.

To prove that he was magically protected from harm the gods hurled spears at Baldur and struck him with swords. They were pleased when they saw that none of these weapons harmed him. However, Loki found out from Frigg that the mistletoe had not made the vow not to harm the young god of summer. He went to an elven smith with a

sprig of the fateful plant and forced him to shape it into a
magical arrow. The dark god then took this to the blind
Hodur and said to him, 'Why not join the merry game.
Here let me place this arrow in your bow and point it at
your brother Baldur.'

Unwittingly duped by the evil Loki the blind god aimed
the bow at Baldur and let fly the deadly mistletoe arrow. It
struck the young god in the heart and he fell dying.
Eventually Loki confessed to his murderous deed and, by
condemnation of the gods, was chained to a rock above
which a snake spat venom on to his face, burning him in
terrible agony. This was his punishment for all eternity for
the murder of the Sun God.

The Forces of Light and Darkness
Those of you who have studied the pagan myths will
recognize in this faery tale the eternal conflict between the
powers of darkness and light. In this case it is the young god
of the summer sun who is killed by the deity representing
the dark season of winter. The sun symbolically dies at
midwinter when it sinks to its lowest point in the sky and its
power wanes. Slowly it rises again and is reborn in full glory
at the high point of the Midsummer Solstice. The ancient
people celebrated these natural events with rituals depicting
death and rebirth with priests and priestesses enacting the
role of the gods in a cosmological drama of the changing
seasons.

Baldur was the Norse version of the dying god whose
death refertilizes the earth. The story of his murder can be
duplicated in the myths of other pagan lands. We have the
god Adonis in Greece who was ritually killed by a wild boar
and passed to the underworld. After the season of his death
(winter) had passed he was reborn and the wild flowers
bloomed once more. In Ancient Egyptian mythology we
have the story of Osiris who is murdered by his twin brother
Set in a symbolic battle between the forces of good and evil.

Sir James Frazer in his classic work of anthropology and
folklore, *The Sacred Bough* (MacMillan, London) has written

extensively of this pagan motif. He tells of the sacred grove
of the goddess Diana at Nemi which was guarded by a
priest who used the title Rex Nemorensis or the King of the
Woods. In the grove of the goddess was a mighty tree of
which no branch might be broken for it was taboo. Only a
runaway slave was allowed to break off the sacred boughs of
the tree. If he managed to do this he could challenge the
guardian priest of the grove to single combat. If then he
managed to kill the old priest then the slave automatically
took his place as the hierophant of the mysteries of Diana.

Earlier in this book we have seen the rites of human and
animal sacrifice which surrounded the cult of Odin. This
same theme dominates the life of his son Baldur and in
many cases it seems as if the two gods are identical, merely
old and young aspects of the one deity sharing a common
bond of family and bloodletting. Certainly Dr William
Chaney's theories concerning the descent of the Anglo-
Saxon kings from Odin and their mysterious deaths
resembling ritual killings (an idea also explored in great
depth by the late Dr Margaret Murray of University
College, London) together with the ancient legend of divine
priest kings such as Rex Nemorensis, suggest a very old
religious or magical tradition coming down through the
centuries from the dawn of pre-history.

The Norns

Although it was Odin who was said to have received the
arcane wisdom of the runes hanging on the World Tree, the
Norse folk often associated the magical alphabet with the
powers of fate or destiny. This was called *wryd* in Old
Scandinavian and was the province of three goddesses
known as the Norns. These goddesses were three sisters
who weaved the fate of men on their looms. In Old English
the words weave, destiny and fortune were often associated
with each other in significant sentences which suggest some
occult (i.e. hidden) meaning is implied by the writer or
speaker.

After the conversion of the pagans to Christianity the

Norns survived as folklore memories of the three Fates, as
the ugly sisters in the pantomime *Cinderella* and in *Sleeping
Beauty* as the wicked witch with the poisoned spinning
wheel. Perhaps the most melodramatic representation of
these old Nordic goddesses is the three witches on the
blasted heath in Shakespeare's play *Macbeth*. He describes
them as 'weird sisters' who could foretell the truth in the
tradition of the pagan Norse seeresses.

In the mythology of the Northern folk the Norns were
known by their personal names of Urd, Verdanki and
Skuld. They personified the past, the present and the future
respectively. They were therefore invoked by the Rune
Masters before they divined the future by casting the runic
letters. The Norns also guarded the Yggdrasill or World
Tree which supports the earth. Every morning they poured
a libation of mead over its roots so that its leaves would stay
green. From this libation comes the honey dew which drips
on the earth and is stored by the bees. The Norns had in
their service fair maidens who materialized in dreams to
impart advice and guidance. These maids also had the task
of finding willing mothers for unborn babies to incarnate in.

It would seem that the personification of the Norns
resembled in many ways the triple aspect of the Great
Goddess which is found in nearly every pagan religion; the
maiden, the mother and the old crone. Urd was said to be
very old and looked backward over her shoulder as old
people often do. Verdanki was a young girl and gazed
straight ahead into the present. Lastly, Skuld was said to be
veiled and had an unopened scroll on her lap which
contained the secrets of the future. Her description sounds
very much like that of the High Priestess card in the gypsy
Tarot pack which is sometimes used for fortune-telling. In
the occult teachings of the Tarot – which have nothing to do
with their usage as a way of predicting coming events – the
card of the High Priestess or Papess symbolizes inspiration,
memory and divine prophecy. She is the medium through
which the Gods or archetypal forces speak to the material
world.

Magical Uses of the Runes

Although today we principally regard the runes as a method of divination, in the past they possessed a multiplicity of magical uses. There were birth runes, health runes, death runes, battle runes, fertility runes, weather runes, love runes and cursing runes. Much of the old runic knowledge has been lost to us today but from archaeological sources we can rediscover the uses of the runes in magic and daily life.

They were frequently used to ward off grave robbers from the burial mounds of important tribal personages such as chiefs and high priests. It was stipulated that these protecting runes had to be carved 'not by day and not by iron'. This seems a rather odd superstition but, like most, it is embedded in magical commonsense (even if that seems a contradiction in terms to some people). The hours of darkness was the obvious time to practise necromantic rites and iron was the only metal which could frighten away departed spirits or the faery folk. Therefore its use was forbidden in or around burial places.

This belief dates back to the early days when the people who used iron conquered the tribes who still boasted bronze weapons and tools. The Bronze Age folk – a small, dark skinned and hairy people – were regarded by the invaders as faeries and the superstitious said that they were scared of the magic metal iron. (Possibly for a good, practical reason for iron can slice through the soft metal of a bronze sword blade.) Hence grew up the tradition that faeries or demons could be destroyed by iron which they mortally feared to touch.

Runes of War

Staying with weapons of war we find that runes were often engraved on swords. An iron sword excavated on the Isle of Wight had inscribed on its blade in runic letters the legend 'Woe to the weapons of the foe'. It also had carved in rune its rather bloodchilling name 'Increase to Pain' which is a pretty accurate description of its use in battle to deal death and injury to the enemy. Another example of sword runes are to be found on a broken blade dredged up from the River Thames. It is over two feet in length and engraved along it are the twenty-eight letters of a runic alphabet and the name of its owner.

An ancient scabbard unearthed at Tonsberg bears the runic inscription 'servant of the god'. It does not name him but we can feel sure that the deity referred to is the god of war, Tiw. On a buckle found near the sword was carved the motto 'I dedicate to the god' which suggests that the weapon was either a sacrificial sword or belonged to a *berserker* who dedicated the souls of his victims to Odin. On a short sword from Kragehul the warrior's name has been carved in runes together with the debatable words 'I bring luck'. It certainly would not bring luck to those who died by its blows.

Runes of Escape

Another use for runes was to escape from your enemies if you were captured after a battle. The Christian historian Bede, writing in 679 c.e., tells of a young Northumbrian captive who slipped his fetters and escaped. When he was recaptured he was asked in Old English 'hwae-oer he pa alysendlecam rune cuoe an pa stafs mid him awritene haefde?' Translated this means 'Do ye know of the loosening runes and do you have the [magical] letters written about you.' Evidence that this was a popular form of runic magic is given by the words of the old god Odin himself who says 'This fourth [runic] skill I know. If men put fetters on my limbs I chant such a charm that will let me escape from them.'

In an Old English charm the user of runes is also told by the hooded god, 'If you wish to go to your king or any other man then bear these runic staves. Each will be gracious and kind to you.'

Runes in Norse Sagas

Runes it seems had unlimited magical powers as the following extracts from the Norse saga illustrate.

Runes of war now thee,
if great thou wilt be,
cut them on hilt of hardened sword,
some on the brand's back,
some on its shining side,
twice the name Tiw therein.

Sea runes good at need,
learnt for ship's saving,
for the good health of the swimming horse;
on the stern cut them,
cut them on the rudder blade,
and set flame the shaven oar,
how so big the sea hills,
how so big the blue beneath,
hail from the main and then
comest thou home.

Word runes learn ye well
if thou wilt that no man,
pay back grief for the grief gavest,
wind thou these, cast thou these
all about you,
At the Thing where folk throng,
until the doom faring.

Of ale runes know the wisdom
if thou wilt another man's wife
should not betray thine heart that trusteth;
cut them on mead horn,
on the back of each hand
and nicked upon the nail.

Help runes shalt thou gather
if skill thou woulds't gain
to loosen chold from low-lain mother;
cut they be in hands hollow,
wrapped the joints round about,
call for the good folks gainsome help.

Learn the bough rune's wisdom
if leechlore thou lovest
and wilt wot about wounds searching,
on the bank they be scored,
on the buds of trees
whose boughs look eastward ever.

Thought runes shalt thou deal with,
if thou wilt be of all men,
fairest souled, right and wise
those creded, those first cut,
those took first to heart.

On the shield were they scored
that stands before the Shining God,
on Early-Waking's oar,
on All Knowing's hoof,
on the wheel which runneth under
Regnir's chariot,
on Sleipnir's jaw teeth,
on the sleigh traces,
on the rough bear's paw,
on Bragi's tongue,
on the wolf's claw,
on the eagle's bill,
on bloody wings,
and bridge's end,
on loosing palms
and pity's path.

On glass, on gold
and goodly silver,
in wine and wort
and the seat of the witch wife,
on Gungir's point
and Grani's bosom,
on the Norn's snail
and the neb of the night owl.

All these so cut
were shaven and sheared
and mingled with hold mead
and sent upon wide ways enow,
some abide with the elves,
some abide with the Aesir
or with the wise Vanir
or some still hold the
sons of mankind.

These be the book runes
and the runes of good help,
and all the ale runes
and the runes of much might
To whom so they may avail
unbewildered, unspoilt.
They are wholesome to hear,
thine thou with these then,
when thou hast heard their lore,
till the Gods end thy life days.

Volsunga Sage

This poem illustrates the many and varied magical uses
of runes, most of which have been unfortunately lost to us
today and are only just being rediscovered. Further
information on the many uses of the magical runes is given
in the following epic poem which is said to have been
composed by Odin for the guidance of his disciples the
Rune Masters.

Know how to cut them,
know how to read them,
know how to stain them,
know how to evoke them,
know how to send them –
the Runes!

Better not to ask them to overpledge,
as a gift demands a gift,
better not to slay,
than to slay too many.

The first charm I know
is unknown to all of any human kind,
'Help' it is named
for help it gives
in hours of anguish
and in sorrow.

I know a second –
that those who would
be leeches must learn.

I know a third –
in battle if need be great,
it blunts the swords of
enemies so there are
no wounds.

I know a fourth –
which frees me quickly
if foes should bind me first,
and chant know I
that breaks fetters,
burst bonds.

A fifth – know I,
no crow hunts,
no spear kills,
no stone hurts.

I know a sixth –
if runes are cut
to harm me,
the spell is turned –
the hunter harmed not I.

I know a seventh rune,
if a hall blazes around
my bench mates,
though hot the flames
they feel nought.

I know an eighth –
if hate festers in
a warrior's heart,
my spell will calm him.

I know a ninth –
when need of it,
to shelter my ship in winter's storm,
the wind it calms,
the sea it puts to sleep.

I know a tenth rune –
if spirits trouble I work;
they wander afar,
unable to find form or home.

I know an eleventh –
when I lead in battle
and unwounded go to war,
unscathed I return.

I know a twelfth –
when I see aloft a tree
a corpse swing from a rope,
then I cut and paint runes
so the man walks,
speaks with me.

I know a thirteenth –
if I cast runes,
no warrior dies in battle
or falls by the sword.

I know a fourteenth –
that few know,
if I tell a troop of
warriors about the Old Ones,
gods and elves
I can name them all.

I know a fifteenth –
sung to the Gods it
gives power to men,
prowess to elves,
foresight to all by
Odin's gift.

I know a sixteenth –
that binds the hearts
and charms the young girls
releasing love.

I know a seventeenth rune –
that is never told,
a secret hidden from all,
except my love in my arms
and my sister.

Misuse of the Runes

This impressive list of magical powers has a hidden sting in
its tail. One line says 'Better not to ask then overpledge, as a
gift demands a gift'.

At first glance perhaps innocent words – or are they
really? It is in fact a subtle warning not to misuse the magic
of the runes. Ask only for what you need because if you are
greedy the powers-that-be will exact from you a tribute
which you may not willingly pay. It is an old belief, based
on cold fact, that if you are too successful in life or too lucky
then something you love will be taken from you by the gods
as the price for your success.

Such a belief is at the heart of the medieval tales
concerning magicians who allegedly made pacts with the
Devil in exchange for material wealth and happiness. At the
conclusion of the bargain the magus, no matter how skilled
he might be in theurgy, always loses and is forced
reluctantly to mortgage his soul to the powers of darkness.
As intelligent and educated people we no longer believe in
the Christian bogeyman who at the witching hour rides up
on a scarlet horse to claim our mortal spirit. However, such
a belief in the untrustworthy gods and the sacrifices

required of those who dabbled with the hidden forces of nature is essentially pagan and predates the fairy tales of Christianity by many thousands of years. It is the ancient law encapsulated in the superstitious words of the wise who seeing someone inherit money say 'No good will come of it'. The tragic circumstances which often surround winners of large sums on the football pools prove the truth of this old adage.

Also in the verses above is the chilling phrase 'Better not to slay than to slay too many'. This refers to the negative aspect of the runes as an instrument of magical murder. However, any one foolish enough to use the runes for this purpose will soon encounter that other ancient law of magic that curses rebound three times over on the sender. This may not happen immediately but eventually the person who misuses the runes – or indeed any form of practical occultism – will have to face the severe consequences of his or her impulsive act. Nature has a way of dealing with those mere mortals who set themselves up as judge and jury over their fellow human beings and it is not a very pleasant fate to suffer.

On a lighter note, it is worth noting that not all runic inscriptions were of a magical significance. Sad to relate there were a few brave individuals who used them for less exalted purposes. When Viking raiders, under the leadership of Rognvaldr Kali, invaded the Orkneys in 1151 c.e. they left behind runic graffiti in the prehistoric burial mound of Maes Howe. It records that a great treasure was carried off from the place by the invading troops. In 1153 the Viking wanderers returned to the island and carved more runes telling of a snow storm which stopped them sailing and how two of their number went insane.

CHAPTER FIVE

THE MAGICAL POWER OF THE RUNES

Magic is probably the most misunderstood word in the human language. If you do not believe that statement ask your friends and work mates what the word means to them. Their answers will be revealing and show just how low the true magical arts have degenerated since their pagan heyday.

Today, magic is associated in the minds of the general public with party conjurers producing rabbits out of top hats, wicked witches waving toytown wands in pantomimes or obscene rites in lonely country churchyards. Each of these images is a modern *cliché* and none of them is in any way representative of true magic or the people who practise it. In the past one did not have to explain what magic was to the majority of people. They encountered it and its effects in everyday life. It was accepted without question that there were certain people who were apart from the common herd, different in a way which could only be understood if you accepted that the material world and the realms of spirit were aspects of one unity. These people possessed strange powers and had unusual knowledge; they could see into the future, read minds and even manipulate the elemental forces of nature. Their powers could be used for evil but in the majority of cases they were respected members of the community who could be called upon to help those in need.

Today we have invented a brand new technical terminology to describe these powers which our ancestors took for granted. We call them extra-sensory perception, parapsychology, precognition, out-of-the-body experiences and telekinesis. Even our feeble attempts to rationalize these powers by giving them pseudo-scientific names cannot disguise how little we really know about them. Nowadays a scientifically educated psychic researcher or 'parapsychologist' would laugh at you if you insisted on describing his field of study as 'magic' or 'magical' but it was so regarded by our forebears and who is to say they were wrong to do so?

Denial of the Pagan View

In earlier chapters the shamanistic tradition has been described. It is a magico-religious belief system which, at first glance, seems to belong to a backward phase of human history when dark superstition and cruel barbarism ruled the lives of humanity. In fact this concept of our pagan past is one that has been forced upon us by conditioning. An insidious and sinister form of conditioning which is inherent in our educational system, which colours the view of the outside world presented to us each morning by the newspapers and on the evening television news. A conditioning process which permeates the scientific and technological establishment and distorts the real truth about the relationship between humans and their physical environment.

Those spiritual anarchists, the shamans, were not conditioned by any man-made force seeking to manipulate their vision of the outside reality. Unlike ourselves they had not been subjected to the theories of Sir Isaac Newton or the philosophy of Descartes who conceived the Universe according to a mechanical model which had been constructed by an omnipotent, supreme creator in the manner of a Swiss watch. Since Newton it has been the traditional scientific stance to separate matter from spirit and this reached the height of its absurdity in the Victorian era of rationalism when spirit was finally denied and rejected.

The scientific establishment rejected the pagan view that the Earth is a living organism, that all life in the Universe is permeated by the creative energy of the Life Force and that everything that exists is part of a greater oneness. The pagans knew and accepted this fundamental fact just as they knew and accepted magic. Their belief in the essential oneness of life and the shamans' concept of the Earth as a living entity are graphically illustrated by the following quotation extracted from the works of a medieval pagan philosopher Basilius Valentinus.

> The Earth is not a dead body but is inhabited by the spirit that is its life and soul. All created things draw their strength from the Earth spirit. This spirit is life, it is nourished by the stars and it gives nourishment to all living things it shelters in its womb.

These are words which would have been easily recognized by the oldtime shaman or Rune Master. Even today they would be acceptable to the surviving magicians of the various ethnic races who still cling tenaciously to the Old Ways despite the spiritual coercion of the missionaries and the material inducements of multi-national companies who have made it their goal to enlighten our brethren of the Third World.

Rejection of Rationalism

Today, when so many people have found the technological dream crumbling around us in crime, vandalism and the pollution of the earth, the old shamanistic ideas are once more beckoning us in the West. The Newtonian-Cartesian-Darwinian theories are being ruthlessly examined and found to be wanting. As the American writer and philosopher Gary Snyder has said recently, it is time at this crucial period in human history to return to the roots of our religious origins. Awareness of what we are doing to our environment by increased industrialism is forcing a new look to be given to the accepted values which arose with the Cartesian philosophy. Snyder has pointed out that a book such as *Black Elk Speaks*, written by a North American shaman, is recognized by many people today as the testament of a spiritual philosophy which predates Judeo-Christianity and the Hindu-Buddhist religion by many thousands of years. It is a philosophy which teaches that humanity cannot separate itself from its physical environment or the matters of the spirit. Each is a reflection of the great oneness which the ancient shamans recognized and tuned into in order to gain their magical powers.

These magical powers belong to a world which has been largely ignored during the last 200 years of material rationalism. Today a few pioneering scientists, such as Dr Fritjof Capra, who has taught us a new system of metaphysical science based on mystical physics, are opening our eyes to a new non-mechanical theory of the universe. We are rediscovering the old shamanistic view of the cosmos and realizing that all life is an eternal, flowing movement of change and transformation, a cosmic dance of the heavens. The universe can be perceived as the final manifestation of an ultimate reality pattern. It is sustained by a unifying essence with a central function to manifest in myriad forms, which come into being, evolve, disintegrate and are then rebuilt in an everlasting cycle of existence.

The Central Truths

At various stages in human history this central truth has either been lost or misunderstood. Our present materialistic age is one of these dark periods. In the past the priesthood, who were the guardians of magical knowledge, knew that the mass of people had largely lost the ability to conceive of the oneness of all life (although a few initiates like the shamans still retained the knowledge). Because of this, three levels of religious expression were developed and humanity began to visualize the Godhead on three levels of understanding.

These were: *The Supreme Creative Principle* – pure, asexual, transcendental energy, sometimes simply referred to as the Life Force. *The Creative Duality* – the Life Force manifesting symbolically as a God and Goddess representing the masculine and feminine aspects of the human psyche. *The*

Archetypes – magical images of the God and Goddess as mythological deities, racial heroes and cultural teachers. The Nordic, Celtic, Roman, Greek, Egyptian and Hindu religions are based on the latter concept and feature gods who, at some early period of the culture's history, were real people living on earth. The Archetypes, according to the Swiss psychologist Dr Carl Jung, represent fundamental human qualities and desires which appear in dreams, myths, visions and folklore.

It should be understood that these Archetypes are subjective personifications of the Supreme Creative Principle of Life Force. However, some occult philosophers claim that they can possess a separate reality outside the realms of human imagination. They claim that the gods are visualized by their human worshippers with such intense concentration that they can become a focus for natural forces seeking manifestation on the material plane. The famous occultist Dion Fortune said that a god is an artificial thought-form built up over long periods of time by successive generations. When the magician or shaman visualizes the image of the god in his or her mind it is the corresponding aspect of his or her nature which gives it power and form.

That the various gods and goddesses invoked in ritual magic (and that includes, for the purpose of this book, the magic of the runes) possess a separate existence as artificial thought forms or elementals is an idea explored by the writer Hzhak Bentov. He even describes the *modus operandi* of creating a god. Bentov imagines a rock in a desert. This inanimate (yet not 'dead' as we understand the term) object has a low level of consciousness. Its threshold of conscious awareness is stimulated by contact with small animals in the vicinity who regard the rock as a protector against the elements and bigger animals. When a human being travels through the desert who is sensitive to Nature he or she finds that there is something 'different' about the stone. If this person is of a culture which follows the animistic old religion, or is sympathetic to such influences, his or her awe of the rock may turn into direct worship of it as a cult object and the habitat of a friendly (or in some cases unfriendly) spirit. This attention boosts the rock's embryonic consciousness even further and eventually the spirit of the stone is transformed into a god.

Manifestations of the Life Force

The belief in spirits which reside in stones is worldwide and can best be experienced in the practices of the Toraja tribe who are scattered across the islands of the Indonesian archipelago. They have set up huge megalithic monuments which today are 'fed' with pig blood but in the past were honoured by human sacrifices. Some of the strange reports of 'supernatural' happenings in the vicinity of European stone circles may be explained by Bentov's theories. Certainly the old idea that stone is an inactive, solid mass has been revised by the latest discoveries in physics which suggest that it is a complex energy structure with many amazing secrets to offer us.

What Bentov is describing in his story of the rock in the desert is the creation of an elemental, faery or nature spirit which is associated with the manifestation of the Life Force through organic matter. These energy forces have been worshipped in the past as minor gods or the spirit guardians of sacred wells, trees, standing stones, lakes and rivers. Such forces have the ability to tune in to the human mind and cause it to interpret them in archetypal images. An example of this process was given to the author by the late W.E. Butler. Visiting an ancient site he saw a small sphere of light hovering over one of the stones. From his experience as a practising occultist he recognized this phenomena as the manifestation of a nature spirit. His companion, who was not clairvoyantly trained and lacked any magical knowledge, also saw the spirit. However, she described it as taking the traditional shape of a faery as depicted in childrens' story books. This experience suggests that in some unknown way we are conditioned to receive aspects of the spiritual reality in specifically constructed archetypal forms. It may also offer an explanation for the modern U.F.O. phenomenon which may have very little to do with close encounters with little green men from Mars but a lot to do with the faery kingdoms and the so-called 'dragon power' which occultists and dowsers say is channelled across the countryside between prehistoric sites along the mysterious ley lines.

The Multi-visioned View

The theory of the universe described above coincides with the recent research work completed by two leading physicists, Karl Pribham of the Stanford University in the United States and Davil Bolm of London University. They allege that our brains mathematically construct what we call reality by interpreting frequencies from a level of primal existence which transcends time and space. This archetypal reality pattern they liken to a universal hologram (i.e. a type of photograph that produces a three dimensional image). They further suggest that phenomena such as magic, precognition, telepathy, time warps, ESP and mystical experience are an aspect of the primal reality and occur when certain people tune in, either accidentally or consciously, to the Universal Matrix which sustains the cosmic hologram.

We seem to have come a long way from the meaning of magic; but not really, for the shaman or rune magician are both examples of people with the above average ability to tune in, either accidentally or consciously, to the Univeral Matrix or spirit world and reactivate those powers of the mind which lie dormant in most other members of the human race. The shaman or rune magician is a multi-visioned entity in contrast to the average person in Western technological society who suffers from that blindness of the spirit which the poet William Blake described as 'single vision'.

Writing recently in the popular American science magazine *Omni*, Kenneth Brower speculated on exactly why humanity seems to have lost its collective footing on the path to progress by means of technological supremacy over the forces of Nature. He thinks that the Judeo-Christian edict in the Bible instructing human beings to increase and multiply in order to subdue Nature and the animal kingdom is one of the root causes of our modern predicament. Brower believes, like the old shamans, that our attitude to the earth was far healthier when we were pagans and believed spirits resided in everything, when humans and animals were on equal terms and trees had to be placated before cutting. In fact, Brower is advocating the multi-visioned view of the natural world as opposed to the single vision.

The Sixth Sense

It is a well known fact that we use only a small percentage of our total available brain power. A great deal of its potency lies submerged in the shadows of the unconscious mind. In prehistoric times it is certain that humanity was far more developed on the intuitive level than we are today. The sensory organs of sight, smell, touch, taste and hearing were far more sharpened as befits primitive men who hunted for their living and faced daily danger from wild animals and other humans who would have cheerfully killed them without compassion.

Gradually, as humanity became more civilized and moved into an era of towns, villages and cities, the so-called sixth sense – the intuitive part of the brain – ceased to function and slowly its powers degenerated. They survived in flashes of inspiration, psychic visions in times of stress or prophetic dreams. This process occurred over a long period of time but has accelerated in our own society during the last 200 years due to our rapid industrialization and retrograde retreat from natural life styles. Some members of the human race (not only in the ethnic areas of the world isolated from the malefic influences of the industrial society) have managed to preserve the magical multi-vision despite pressures from the single-visioned technocrats to conform to the status quo.

Social Conditioning
Young children are naturally psychic and will often talk of
invisible playmates. Such talk is usually dismissed by
unenlightened parents as the product of infantile
imaginations. In fact, children who repeatedly tell tales
about faeries or angels may be treated as pathological liars
or mentally deficient. Faced with such a prospect children
soon learn to stay silent for to speak openly of such natural
happenings is to invite the ridicule and contempt of grown-
ups. This process is reinforced when the child reaches
school age for there is no place in our modern education
system for the dreamer, poet or visionary. Education today
(except in some progressive schools where the pupils are
allowed, indeed encouraged, to develop their artistic and
creative talents) is geared to producing nicely conditioned
zombies who will become the technologists and factory
fodder of our brave new industrial world.

In the past no such inhibitions were placed on the person
who claimed to have visions or had the power to make
things happen. They were regarded as important people
whose natural awareness of the spirit world was a valuable
contribution to the community. When Christianity became
the dominant religion of Western Europe (and it did not do
so without a long struggle with paganism which lasted
hundreds of years) the psychic and the magician became
the outcasts of society.

Invoking the Power of the Runes
Returning to the special magical powers of the runic
alphabet – how can the average person today, who wishes to
escape from the limits of single vision existence, tap the
occult power of the runes?

Rune magic, like all practical occult techniques, can be
dangerous. Great caution is required and the runes should
never be treated as an amusing parlour game, an
entertainment or a means of making quick money. If you
regard them in this light then disaster is bound to follow
your attempts to unravel their secrets. These ancient

magical sigils do not give up their knowledge easily, as the great god Odin discovered as he hung on the World Tree long ago.

In occult workings the runes can be used, as any magical alphabets are, to add extra power to the ritual or spell. Before using the runes you should invoke Odin who represents the power inherent in the runic characters. A suggested invocation is given below for your guidance although readers may care to make up their own.

> Odin, upholder of the Sun and the ocean,
> Supporter of the Moon, All father!
> Possesser of arcane wisdom,
> Lord of the Faery Hosts,
> Wild Hunter of the Midwinter sky,
> Ruler of the Underworld and the crossroads,
> I [*insert your name*] invoke and
> call upon thee to aid me in the Great Work.
>
> At the time I seek [*state your
> intention*] with your help and
> through the wisdom of the magical
> runes which are under thy protection.

During this invocation visualize the god standing in front of you. His physical description is given in Chapter One.

Healing Ritual

As an example, let us imagine that our rune magician has decided to perform a healing ritual using the runes for a friend who is ill in hospital. After the invocation to Odin the magician writes the person's name on a piece of paper in runes as follows.

SALLY   BOWLES

As the runic alphabet we are using does not include runic letters for Y and E we can merely substitute a magical symbol representing the sun for these missing letters.

Below the patient's name the magician writes down the name and location of the hospital also in runes.

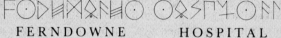

FERNDOWNE   HOSPITAL

NORTHAMPTON

Then a petition to Odin (who is the Nordic version of Mercury and therefore the god of healing) and his son Baldur, who represents the life-giving rays of the sun, is written in runes. A suggested wording is given below but again the reader can use his or her own version.

> Mighty Odin, Lord of the North Wind,
> Baldur, shining light-bringer,
> beloved of the Gods,
> I [*insert name*] ask for the
> power of healing to be sent
> to Sally Bowles at Ferndowne
> Hospital, Northampton.
> That she may be cured of
> [*insert health condition*]
> and restored fully to vitality and good health.
> I ask this boon, not for myself
> but for her that the will of the
> Gods be done and the law of the
> Norns be respected.
> By the power of wind, fire and water
> and in the holy names of Odin, Baldur,
> Freyja and Thor.

This petition is then read out in a clear, strong voice and the piece of paper it is written on is then burnt to ashes in the flame of a blue or white candle. Blue and white are both healing colours.

As the paper burns the magician may visualize a ray of blue light emanating from the forehead just above the bridge of the nose, which is the site of the psychic Third Eye and the physical pineal gland, towards the magical image of Odin which has been materialized earlier in the ritual.

When this has been achieved, the magician thanks Odin and Baldur for their help. Again a suggested working is given below.

I [insert own name],
thank thee Odin, grim lord of the dead
and guardian of the runes,
I [insert own name],
thank thee bright Baldur,
youngest of the North Gods.
Before ye depart to thy icy realms
beyond the Northern Lights,
I offer ye this sacrifice,
freely given, without pain or death
to any living creature.

A symbolic gesture of personal sacrifice is then made. This could be the burning of a piece of hair, a drop of blood drawn from the forefinger of the left (pagan) hand or the pouring of a libation of mead or wine.

As soon as this symbolic act has been performed visualize the image of Odin slowly fading from view into nothingness. Before you start you may wish to consecrate the room you are working in. You can do this by imagining a circle of blue light surrounding it. This symbolic barrier prevents the ritual being disturbed by outside or negative influences. If required this circle of protection can be reinforced by evoking the elemental guardians of the north, south, east and west. Details of such evocations are given in my previous book *Candle Burning: Its Occult Significance* (The Aquarian Press, Wellingborough).

As an added (magical) bonus the healing ritual detailed above should be performed on a Wednesday (Woden's day) which is sacred to the god Odin. If possible the moon should be waning i.e. decreasing towards the new moon.

Many occultists have an aversion to working magic when the moon is in this waning phase. This is a rather short-sighted viewpoint for on a waning moontide unwanted influences and illnesses can be effectively banished. When you should traditionally *never* work magic or indulge in occult activities of a practical nature is the period of three days before the new moon known as 'the dark of the moon'. In old folklore this time was allegedly ruled by the vampire goddess Lilith who attacked men sexually and was the queen of hobgoblins, ghosts and demons. She is of course the dark aspect of the Great Mother Goddess of prehistoric times who has always been feared by the followers of the patriarchal religions.

The Powers of the Gods

Different Nordic gods and goddesses can be invoked in rune magic for different purposes. Some of these are listed below together with their sacred days and planetary influences.

God/Goddess	Day	Planet	Rulership
Odin	Wednesday	Mercury	Healing, wisdom and knowledge
Freyja	Monday	Moon	Intuition, clairvoyance and psychism
Tiw	Tuesday	Mars	Courage and strength
Thor	Thursday	Jupiter	Wealth and material prosperity
Frigg	Friday	Venus	Love, fertility and childbirth
The Norns	Saturday	Saturn	Fate, destiny and luck
Baldur	Sunday	Sun	Healing, self-confidence and family

Descriptions of these deities for visualization purposes can usually be found in any good reference book from the public library on Norse mythology.

Norse Months and Festivals

As well as the days of the week the old Norse people had different names for the months than the ones we use today, which are based on Roman usage introduced when Britain was conquered by Julius Caesar and his legions. The Norse month names and the major sacred festivals are as follows.

Norse	Roman	Festival	Date
Wolfmoon	December	Night of the Mothers	21st
		Twelfth Night	31st
Snowmoon	January	Blessing of the Plough	1st
Horning	February	Festival of the Family	14th
Lenting	March	Summer Finding (Equinox)	21st
Ostara	April		
Merrymoon	May	May Day	1st
Fallow	June	Midsummer	21st
Harvest	August	Harvest Festival	28th
Shedding	September	Winter Finding (Equinox)	21st
Hunting	October		
Fogmoon	November	Heroes Day	11th

Amulets and Talismans

As well as using runes for invocations as a magical alphabet they can also be engraved on amulets and talismans. These can easily be worn as items of personal jewellery without fear of comment. An amulet is used to ward off negative influences and dispel bad luck. The talisman on the other hand is used like a magical magnet to attract good influences and positive vibrations to the person who wears it. Under normal circumstances a talisman is consecrated by its maker so that it attracts a specific influence, be it love, good health or money.

In Icelandic pagan magic special runic symbols have been created as talismans to attract various virtues for the benefit of the user. Iceland is still a very pagan country (it was not converted to the Christian religion until the eleventh century c.e.) and these runic charms are very popular. They are even openly on sale in the tourist shop at Reykjavik Airport from where the examples given below originate.

This is a charm used to grant wishes of all kinds.

This charm is used to ward off negative forces and protect the wearer from his or her enemies.

This sigil is used to prevent a rival magician from placing an evil spell on you.

Love charm. If worn around the neck on silver chain this is said to attract the love of the person you most desire.

This is a charm used by Icelanders to attract money and prosperity.

Dress symbol. Write this rune sigil on a piece of paper or engrave it on a twig of birch wood. Place it under your pillow. Your dreams will come true.

This is not the old German Nazi swastika. It is the ancient Nordic magical symbol known as the Hammer of Thor. It is worn by pagan Icelanders who require the divine protection of the thunder god.

A runic cross which may be a Christian innovation for it protects the wearer from ghosts, evil spirits, demons and the faery folk.

The symbol above was widely used by Scandinavian sailors to prevent their ships being sunk in storms. Note the interesting similarity between this runic seal and the design of an anchor.

This last rune can be used to heal all sicknesses of mind, body and spirit. It is dedicated to Odin.

Magical Rings

Another potent use of the runes was on magical rings. In

ancient tales of sorcery these rings were said to be able to make the magus invisible, protect him from evil or let him fly like a bird. Several rune rings have been discovered in recent years.

One, found at a place with the evocative name of Greymoor Hill, boasted thirty runes engraved on its surface. Twenty-seven outside and three powerful ones inside. Another rune ring found at Bramhan also had thirty runes, divided into three groups: nine, nine and twelve. These are lunar numbers and are associated with the phases of the moon, the Great Mother Goddess and the pagan Old Religion.

Magical rune rings have survived into modern times. One of the leading members of a German magical fraternity in the early twentieth century made a lucrative living by selling bronze rings inscribed with magical incantations written in the runic alphabet. He claimed the rings could protect their owners from illness and even sold them to German troops who were fighting in the trenches of France during the First World War.

CHAPTER SIX

CASTING THE RUNES

Today people frequently consult astrologers, palmists and clairvoyants in attempts to discover what their future holds. In pagan Europe people visited the local rune magician who by casting the runes divined the future and advised his or her clients of the portents revealed in the mystic pattern of Odin's alphabet.

Divination or predicting the future is a psychic art as old as humanity itself. It is one of the basic urges of humankind to want to know what will be the shape of things to come. It is also an integral part of the shamanistic tradition which we have examined throughout this book as a thread running through runecraft. As we have seen the ability to look into the future was regarded as a gift from the gods to the shaman who passed it on to the tribe.

One can easily imagine that in a society where the ability to survive from day to day was governed by intuition and commonsense any person capable of predicting the unpredictable would be much in demand. As tribal society became more complex divination took on the form of a social science and eventually was integrated into the authoritarian State priesthoods which replaced the shamans. The seer was regarded as a very important person in the court of a tribal or national king or queen. His or her role in fact preceded the modern employment of social scientists and professional trend watchers hired by governments and corporations to predict future social trends.

Shamanistic Techniques

The training of a seer was a long and arduous ordeal. It involved long periods of hard work under the guidance and control of an initiated shaman. Novices were first taught self-discipline which is the key to successful prediction. They were taught the hidden meaning of Nature and Her many wonderful secrets. They were also taught to divine portents in the hunting cry of an owl, see the future in passing storm clouds or visualize coming events by images reflected in a forest lake.

Shamanistic training for seership involved such well-known occult techniques as fasting, abstaining from sex and sleep and many hours of meditation and trance. Only by enduring such hardships of the physical body could the novice seer release the psychic energies within and achieve the necessary amount of self-illumination which brings the required contact with the spirit realm. To obtain this level of extra-sensory awareness the shaman uses trance, ritual drumming, dancing and the partaking of natural drugs such as the red-capped sacred mushroom known as *amanita muscaria*.

Sacred Mushroom

According to shamanistic myths the strange powers of the sacred mushroom were given to humanity by the gods. It is said that Big Raven had caught a whale and could not send it home to his house in the sea. He could not lift the travelling bag which contained all the provisions which the whale needed for the journey. He therefore called upon the Great Spirit to help him in the task. The Spirit said to him, 'Go to the flat place near the sea. There you will find the white stalks with spotted caps. These are the spirits which will help you.' Raven went to the place and the Great Spirit spat on the earth and where its saliva fell up sprang the sacred mushrooms. Raven ate the strange fungi and immediately had the strength to lift the travelling bag so that the whale could be carried home.

During the eating of the *amanita muscaria* the shaman often

sees and communicates with the spirits of the mushroom.
These spirits materialize in a shape not unlike the fungus
itself. They are squat and of a brown leathery complexion
with domed heads, wrinkled faces and thin arms. Their
bodies possess no legs and are rooted in the earth. Often
they ask for homage from the shaman, offerings or tell him
to worship the moon, the hills, rivers or trees. They will
then permit the shaman to see visions of the spirit world or
have a glimpse of the future.

There is ample evidence from both historical and
contemporary accounts that the sacred mushroom can open
up the psychic centres although it is not a method which is
recommended by the author as it can have dangerous side
effects. The following details of the magical use of the sacred
mushroom in a modern context were originally published in
the privately printed newsletter of a pagan group in Wales a
few years ago.

The account related how a small gathering of modern
pagans met at an ancient circle of stones next to a stream in
the countryside. They gathered wood for a fire, lit it and
took the sacred mushroom. They then evoked the
elementals of the earth, the faeries, gnomes and elves.
Slowly they paced around the fire with the women of the
group singing a low, wordless chant.

After about fifteen minutes they saw by the light of the
fire five small figures sitting cross legged in the nearby long
grass. One of the group heard the music of pipes in the
distance. The women then evoked the spirits of the water
and the group heard splashing sounds coming from the
nearby stream and laughter like small children. They were
also the sound of tinkling bells.

While it can be argued by sceptics that these experiences
could be hallucinations created by the use of the
psychedelic fungi it is also a fact that for many thousands of
years the sacred mushroom has been credited with the
power to open up the psychic vision and grant access to the
faery kingdom of the Old Gods.

Runic Divination

Whether or not the magic mushroom was consumed, omens were frequently divined in ancient times by throwing down bundles of arrows or sticks. The future was foretold by the pattern the sticks formed on the ground. The Chinese divinatory system of the I Ching is perhaps the purest form of this type of fortune-telling. The runes are a later and more sophisticated version of the I Ching which combined the pattern made on the ground with mystical symbols.

One of the earliest references to runic divination is given by Tacitus writing of the superstitions prevalent among the German pagan tribes. He says:

> They lop a branch from a fruit tree and cut it into slips, marking them with distinctive signs. Then they scatter the pieces at random on white cloth. An official priest (if it is a matter of tribal importance) or the head of the household (if it is private) prays to the gods and, looking up into the sky, picks up the sticks one at a time and interprets them in accordance with the signs stamped on them.

This method of rune divination has changed little since Tacitus wrote about it nearly 2,000 years ago. However, individual rune casters use different methods. Therefore the ones given in this book may vary from others you may read in some respects, although the basics are the same.

If you decide to cast the runes first choose how you are going to present them. They can be burnt onto small oblong pieces of wood with a hot poker, painted on pebbles or incised on slate tablets. If you are a craftsman or woman used to working on metal they can be engraved on discs of copper, bronze or (if you can afford it) gold. Alternatively, if you are not artistic (and many of us are not) the runic characters can simply be written in felt pen, crayon or ink on squares of white cardboard.

What do the runes mean in divination? For the assistance of the trainee rune caster their prediction symbolism is given below.

Prediction Symbolism

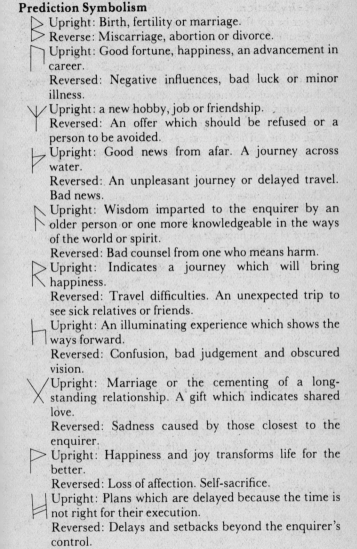

Upright: Birth, fertility or marriage.

Reverse: Miscarriage, abortion or divorce.

Upright: Good fortune, happiness, an advancement in career.

Reversed: Negative influences, bad luck or minor illness.

Upright: a new hobby, job or friendship.

Reversed: An offer which should be refused or a person to be avoided.

Upright: Good news from afar. A journey across water.

Reversed: An unpleasant journey or delayed travel. Bad news.

Upright: Wisdom imparted to the enquirer by an older person or one more knowledgeable in the ways of the world or spirit.

Reversed: Bad counsel from one who means harm.

Upright: Indicates a journey which will bring happiness.

Reversed: Travel difficulties. An unexpected trip to see sick relatives or friends.

Upright: An illuminating experience which shows the ways forward.

Reversed: Confusion, bad judgement and obscured vision.

Upright: Marriage or the cementing of a long-standing relationship. A gift which indicates shared love.

Reversed: Sadness caused by those closest to the enquirer.

Upright: Happiness and joy transforms life for the better.

Reversed: Loss of affection. Self-sacrifice.

Upright: Plans which are delayed because the time is not right for their execution.

Reversed: Delays and setbacks beyond the enquirer's control.

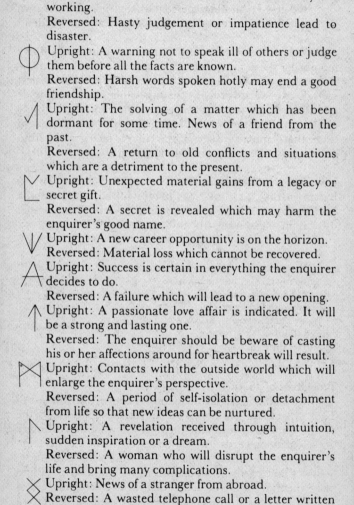

Upright: Caution is required if the enquirer is to succeed in his or her aims. The forces of destiny are working.

Reversed: Hasty judgement or impatience lead to disaster.

Upright: A warning not to speak ill of others or judge them before all the facts are known.

Reversed: Harsh words spoken hotly may end a good friendship.

Upright: The solving of a matter which has been dormant for some time. News of a friend from the past.

Reversed: A return to old conflicts and situations which are a detriment to the present.

Upright: Unexpected material gains from a legacy or secret gift.

Reversed: A secret is revealed which may harm the enquirer's good name.

Upright: A new career opportunity is on the horizon.

Reversed: Material loss which cannot be recovered.

Upright: Success is certain in everything the enquirer decides to do.

Reversed: A failure which will lead to a new opening.

Upright: A passionate love affair is indicated. It will be a strong and lasting one.

Reversed: The enquirer should be beware of casting his or her affections around for heartbreak will result.

Upright: Contacts with the outside world which will enlarge the enquirer's perspective.

Reversed: A period of self-isolation or detachment from life so that new ideas can be nurtured.

Upright: A revelation received through intuition, sudden inspiration or a dream.

Reversed: A woman who will disrupt the enquirer's life and bring many complications.

Upright: News of a stranger from abroad.

Reversed: A wasted telephone call or a letter written which will never be answered.

Upright: A will or legacy bringing benefits to the enquirer or their family.
Reversed: An older person who, if left to their own selfish devices, could become a long-standing burden.

How do you cast the runes? Remember that it took many months for the ancient rune magicians to learn their craft so do not expect very accurate results at first. The easiest method of casting is to take the rune stones you have made and throw them down on the ground in front of you. Only interpret those runes which land facing upwards. Disregard those that cannot be seen. If the rune is facing away from you then use the reversed meanings given above.

Invoking the Guardian

Before casting the runes it is suggested that you mentally invoke the guardian of the runes Odin. A suggested invocation to use is given below.

> Great Odin,
> Master of the secret Runes,
> guide my hands and thoughts
> so that my questions shall
> be answered true and right.
> In the names of Thor, Freyja
> and Baldur,
> and by the magic power of
> wind, fire and water.

The Cross of Thor

Another method of runic divination is known as the Cross of Thor. Using the cards on which you have inscribed the runic characters you shuffle them as you would an ordinary pack of playing cards. As you do so formulate the question you want to ask in your mind.

Select four cards at random from the shuffled pack and place them in the shape of an equal-armed cross in front of you. In the centre of the cross formed by the cards place a fifth one from the pack.

Moving clockwise around the Cross of Thor, rune card number one at the bottom represents the general influences surrounding your enquiry. Card number two on the left side of the cross represents the obstacles which face you. Rune card three, which is opposite to card two on the other side of the cross, illustrates the forces working in your favour. At the top of the cross, rune card four is the short term consequences for you in the runic answer to your question and finally rune card five in the centre is the long term influence on your life by the meaning of the spread.

This form of runic divination is ideally suited for specific important questions which do not require long and complicated answers. However, if you feel that you require a more detailed summary of future trends then the Runic Wheel is recommended which involves twelve runes.

The Runic Wheel

Again the pack of rune cards or tablets is shuffled. Odin is invoked as before and then thirteen cards are dealt from the pack. These may be selected at random throughout the pack or dealt straight off the top in sequence. Once selected the twelve cards are laid out in a circular pattern or wheel before you, starting at the 9 o'clock position and working around anti-clockwise. The thirteenth card you have selected is placed in the middle of the Runic Wheel. At this stage you do not need to be reminded that thirteen is a very important magic number associated with the thirteen moons or months of the old pagan year.

Having laid out your runes they are then interpreted individually and in relation to each other in groups of three. Some rune casters align the Runic Wheel with the twelve houses of the Zodiac which represent different spheres of life. This is a very useful method of divination and the meaning of the astrological houses are given below for reference.

First House. This is the house of interests centred around the person casting the runes, especially health matters. Planetary ruler: Mars.

Second House relates to material possessions, money and

personal security connected with finance. Planetary ruler: Venus.

Third House rules the enquirer's relationship with his or her family, relatives and intimate friends. Also covers letter writing, telephone calls and short journeys. Planetary ruler: Mercury.

Fourth House relates to matters connected with the enquirer's home life, immediate environment and anything which belongs to them. Planetary ruler: the Moon.

Fifth House relates to the creative arts, sport, gambling and other manifestations of the individual's self-awareness. Planetary ruler: the Sun.

Sixth House rules the relationship between the individual and the outside world. Also includes indications of serious illness. Planetary ruler: Mercury.

Seventh House connects with marriage, love affairs and the relationship between the enquirer and members of the opposite sex. If homosexual it covers the enquirers relationship with both sexes.

Eighth House indicates possible gains through legacies or wills. May also indicate the possible nature of the enquirer's own death or that of those closest to him or her. (If reading the runes for someone else this information should be omitted unless specifically requested by the enquirer). Planetary ruler: Pluto.

Ninth House rules travel abroad, legal matters, religion and non-blood relatives such as in-laws. Planetary ruler: Jupiter.

Tenth House. This is the astrological house ruling the enquirer's career and indicates how best he or she can establish themselves in the outside world. Planetary ruler: Saturn.

Eleventh House rules the enquirer's relationship with his or her friends and interests in social clubs, societies or charitable organizations. Also the house of innermost desires and dreams. Planetary ruler: Uranus.

Twelfth House. This final house relates to the secret or hidden life of the enquirer. Also relates to isolation from the world or withdrawals from reality – rules, prisons, hospitals, closed religious orders and service to humanity. Planetary ruler: Neptune.

By using the divinatory meanings of the runes and the special symbolism of the twelve houses of the Zodiac the rune caster can, after much practice and experience, not to mention psychic insight, produce a fairly comprehensive prediction pattern of the future.

CHAPTER SEVEN

RUNIC SURVIVALS

The heyday of the rune magicians was in the so-called Dark
Ages after the Romans left Britain and we were invaded by
Vikings, Danes and Saxon war bands. Our modern vision of
the Vikings is one of uncouth barbarians who raped and
looted their way across England during one of the darkest
periods of our island's history. The truth, as is often the case
with modern accounts of pagan peoples, is somewhat
different. It had been revealed recently through historical
research and archaeological excavations that the Vikings
were a cultivated and civilized race who do not deserve the
bloodthirsty image which popular films and sensational
novels have given them. Their jewellery is second to none in
fine craftsmanship and artistry and the recent excavations
at York have revealed that the Vikings were the merchants
of the ancient world. Rows of shops have been unearthed
where merchants from all over the Continent travelled to
exchange wares and trade in wool, precious metals and
weapons. The Nordic people occupied large areas of
England and left their trademark today in the survival of
local folk customs, place names and even the racial
characteristics of the inhabitants. They administered these
tracts of land right up to the Norman conquest, which was
basically the result of a family squabble between rival
pagan tribes fighting for the English crown.

Anglo-Saxon and Norse England is generally regarded by
historians as a debased, barbaric country. However the
Saxons were capable of exquisite works of art. These
include the famous Kingston brooch found in Kent. Dating

from the seventh century c.e. it consists of a concentric
design relieved by a cruciform pattern decorated with
roundels and bosses. It uses gold, garnet, blue glass and
white sea shell for relief. This brooch is a true example of
Saxon workmanship at its best and proves the lie to the
claims of those who dismiss the Saxon and Norse periods of
English history as the Dark Ages.

Absorption of Paganism

In our study of the magical runes we should also remember
that the transition period from the practice of the pagan
Old Religion and the conversion to Christianity was far
longer than orthodox historians and theologians would have
us believe. It was certainly not a case of waving a magic
wand and everyone became Christian overnight as many
history books suggest. While the aristocracy may have been
convinced of the political power offered by the new religion,
the country folk – who were the real pagans – refused to
accept the teachings from the East and clung tenaciously to
their old beliefs.

Realizing this the Christian priests adapted the old ways
to their religious beliefs and effectively negated them by
absorption. Pope Gregory wrote to one of his British
missionaries in the following words outlining how the Old
Religion could be destroyed from within by his disciples.

> The idols amongst the people should on no account be
> destroyed but the temples themselves should be aspersed with
> holy water, altars to Christ set up in them and relics deposited
> therein. For if these heathen temples are well built they should
> be purified from the worship of demons and dedicated to the
> greater service of God. In this way the people, seeing their
> temples are not destroyed, may abandon their error and flock
> more readily to their accustomed resorts and there may come
> to know and adore the true God.

Such propaganda even influenced the followers of pagan
rune magic. Some were quite happy to accept Jesus as
another aspect of Odin. After all, the new god also hung on

a tree and ritually died for the sins of his tribe. This was an
eternal motif understood by all pagan peoples who knew of
the sacrifice of the divine king who died to fertilize the earth
with his blood. They therefore had no hesitation in
accepting the mother of the Jewish divine king, Mary, as
another aspect of the Great Goddess.

The Dual Faith

During the period of Dual Faith which existed up to the
eleventh and twelfth century c.e. runes became a mystical
alphabet used to describe the life of Jesus and his disciples.
A classic example is the Ruthwell Cross in a churchyard at
Dumfries. This is inscribed with runes telling the story of
the crucifixion intermingled with pagan symbols such as
birds, animals and wild flowers. It also includes scenes from
the nativity, the flight by Mary and Joseph to Egypt, the
baptism of John, the healing of a blind man by the
Nazarene and Mary Magdalene washing his feet.

On a coffin made for St Cuthbert in 698 c.e. runes and
Roman letters are used side by side. Runes are especially
used for the names of Jesus and the four apostles, Matthew,
Mark, Luke and John. This is a survival of the pre-
Christian practice of using the runes for the sacred names of
the gods. That they were still in use for the tomb inscription
of a seventh century Christian holy man proves that their
magical power had not diminished with the coming of the
new religion.

Christian prayers often used pagan incantations, merely
changing the names of the old pagan gods to those of saints
and apostles. The folklorist Alexander Carmichael (1832-
1912) spent a lifetime collecting Gaelic prayers and
blessings still in common usage in the Scottish Highlands
and the Hebrides. Many of these are thinly disguised pagan
incantations for good harvests or the consecration of the
seed. As well as calling on Jesus and the saints the prayers
also invoke St Bride who is a Christianized version of the
Celtic goddess of sacred fires and holy wells, Bridget.
Examples of these prayers can be found in Carmichael's

book *The Sun Dances* (Floris Books, Edinburgh).

In one famous case of this type the Lord's Prayer, written in runes, was used by pagan Saxons as a battle charm. As late as the eleventh century (when historians would have us believe that Christianity was the omnipotent religion of Western Europe and paganism was a forgotten superstition) an Abbot Aelfric was forced to condemn 'outh drycraft oe runstafum' or the use of magic by means of the runes.

Earlier, during the eighth and ninth centuries c.e., some rural graveyards boasted head stones carved with runic prayers to the dead. One of the most amazing examples of the fusion of paganism with Christianity is the famous Franks casket which dates from this period of Dual Faith. It is named after Sir Augustus Franks who presented it to the British Museum in 1867. The casket features representations of Saxon pagan religion alongside scenes from the Bible and both described in the magical alphabet of the runes.

The front of the casket has on its left side an illustration depicting the Saxon god Wayland in his smithy – popularly supposed to be a neolithic burial mound near Uffington earthworks in Berkshire – complete with anvil, hammer and bellows. He holds in his metalworking tongs a human head which is to be made into a skull drinking cup. The headless body of its owner lies beneath the god's anvil. Two female assistants stand nearby and outside a young boy (possibly Wayland's brother Egil) is shown catching geese.

On the right of the casket can be seen the three magi or astrologers kneeling with gifts before the Virgin Mary and her new born baby. Above shines the star over Bethlehem. Each of the pictures is surrounded by a border of runic characters which explains each one.

Healing Charms

It is probable that the secrets of the runes were kept alive by the Anglo-Saxon physicians who practised leechcraft. This

involved the use of magical charms, healing herbs and
incantations which combined pagan and Christian prayers.
An example of a pagan-Christian healing charm is given
below.

> Our Lord Woden rade,
> his foal's foot slade
> down he lighted
> his foal's foot righted,
> bone to bone, flesh to flesh,
> heal in the name of
> Woden, Baldur and Freyja.
> Baldur and Woden
> fared to the wood,
> there was to Baldur's foal
> his foot wrenched,
> then charmed Woden
> as well he knew how,
> as for bone wrench,
> so for limb wrench,
> bone to bone,
> limb to limb
> as if they were glued.

Another example of a Norse Saxon charm derived from
runic magic is the following which was used to cure burns.
It mentions the Norns and the major gods of the Nordic
pantheon.

> Three ladies came out of the east,
> with snow, frost and fire,
> out fire – in frost,
> in the names of Woden, Thor and Loki.

This fusion of pagan and Christian belief illustrates the
struggle in Anglo-Saxon England between the rival faiths. It
was the battle of minds, souls and hearts which reached up
from peasant cottage to the halls of the kings who claimed
descent from Woden. It ended in bloody strife for as soon as

the Church gained political power it suppressed the heretics in its ranks and the unbelievers outside its kingdom who chose to follow different spiritual paths.

Persecution of Pagans

In the late fourteenth century the first major witchcraft trials began and during the next 400 years it is estimated that nearly nine million men, women and children died to satisfy the Church's insane revenge against the pagans. Many innocents were among those who went to their deaths on the pyre or gibbet. Faced with such horrific tortures as the eye gougers, thumb screws and the rack many chose a false confession and a quick death to the prolonged agony of the Inquisition.

Condemnation of the runes as symbols of black magic was a result of the medieval witch hunts. By the end of the Middle Ages rune lore was largely forgotten. The word *rune* had degenerated to mean any magical word or symbol used in a spell or incantation. It was not until the late nineteenth century that runes once more appeared in public consciousness and this was the result of research by German occultists who were trying to revive Teutonic and Norse paganism.

Political Paganism

Many of these occultists identified themselves with various extreme forms of German nationalism. One of these was Dr Benhard Koerner, a member of the Prussian Herald's Office and an expert on the geneology of old German families. Koerner became a member of the Germanen Order in 1912. This was an extreme right wing group combining anti-Semitic politics with occultism and rune magic. It had revived the Mysteries of Odin and its initiates were introduced to the fraternity by a ritual resembling those practised in the pagan temples of pre-Christian Europe. The initiate was told he was a member of a superior race and told to kiss the blade of a sword as a symbolic gesture of allegiance to the Order. One of the first spiritual teachings he was given was the meaning of the magical rune alphabet.

Koerner was a disciple of the famous German occultist Guido Von List whose book *The Secrets of Runes* was a bestseller in European occult circles. Another associate of Koerner was Baron von Sebbottendorf who edited a magazine called *Runen* or *The Rune* devoted to Aryan paganism, rune lore and anti-Jewish propaganda. The Baron purchased a small publishing house in 1918 which was later responsible for printing the magazine *Volkischer Beobachter* which was the official organ of the National Socialist Party. It is certain that Hitler and his cronies were fascinated by the runes and their secret occult powers. He even adopted the rune as the symbol of the feared SS élite troops who effectively ruled occupied Europe.

Today, the worship of the old Norse gods still continues. There are Odinist movements in Germany, Britain, Canada, the United States and Australia. Some advocate extreme right wing politics which suggest a link with the German nationalists and many still practise the ancient art of rune magic.

CHAPTER EIGHT

THE DRUID ALPHABET

In our investigation of the magical powers of the runes we have mentioned the early Celtic alphabet of ogham. This is a Gaelic word derived from the name of the sun god Ogma who was a poet, harper and healer and is said to have invented the ogham script.

Professor Rhys, the noted Celtic historian, states that the word 'ogham' can be translated as 'one skilled in words'. This would seem an accurate description of a person skilled in the occult use of the old Celtic magic. It would also be a good description of the Norse or Saxon rune casters and magicians.

Origins of Ogham Script

Ogham is said by some authorities to have been imported from the East which was the original homeland of the Celtic tribes. The earliest remains of Celtic culture in Europe are dated between 800 and 500 b.c.e. (before common era) and appear in Austria. The Celts emerged from Central Europe as a distinctive race around 1,000 to 800 b.c.e. and would seemed to have originated among the Indo-European peoples of the Asian subcontinent some hundreds of years earlier.

Evidence of the Asiatic origin of the Western European tribes of this period is given by the discovery of a relief from the buried city of Mohenjodaro in the Punjab dating from 2,000 b.c.e. This depicts a horned god with three faces and an erect penis. He sits in a cross-legged yoga position surrounded by animals such as tigers, elephants, goats, oxen, fish, birds and rhinoceros. This Asian deity of fertility can be compared with the depiction of the European Gundestrup cauldron of the Celtic horned god Cernnunos (from the Latin meaning 'the Horned One') who was called the Lord of Animals. They are almost identical in every feature.

It has also been suggested that the prototype of the ogham alphabet was a form of Greek lettering used in Northern Italy a few centuries b.c.e. As we have seen the runes also traditionally originated from that area and were associated with the Etruscan civilization so there seems to be a definite connection between the two alphabets.

According to David Diringer in his *The Alphabet: A Key to the History of Mankind Vol. 1* (Hutchinson, London) the inventors of the ogham script were familiar with the runes. He even goes as far as to say that the ogham and runic alphabets are allied systems of magical writing with a common origin. Professor Rhys however points to Southern Ireland as the birthplace of ogham.

The ogham alphabet consisted of twenty letters – fifteen consonants and five vowels – and seemed to have corresponded to a deaf and dumb type language system. The alphabet was divided into five groups which represented the fingers on the human hand. When not written ogham was employed as a sign language by the user touching his fingers on the nose, forearm or thigh. When writing ogham strokes were used in relation to the stemline on wood or stone in the same way. An example is given below.

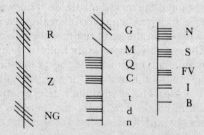

Example of Ogham Script

Druidic Rites

Ogham was taught by the Celtic druids or 'men of the oak trees' who were the priest magicians of the Celts. Despite the many books written about the druids their practices and beliefs are shrouded in myth and mystery. There is even confusion about the correct meaning of their name. The author has accepted the explanation given by the ancient scholar Pliny who said it derives from a Greek word *drus* meaning 'oak tree'. The second syllable is regarded as the corruption of the Indo-European root word *wid* meaning 'to know'. It is possible that the word druid is also allied to the later Saxon *wiccae* meaning 'wise one' which was eventually debased into witch in Middle Age Europe.

Accounts of the druids and their activities by outsiders, such as Julius Caesar, Strabo, Pliny and Tacitus, are distorted and coloured by the writers' prejudices. Caesar was a member of a race who regarded themselves as superior to the 'barbarians' who inhabited Western Europe which they occupied. He therefore did all he could to blacken the image of the Celts and present them as uncivilized savages. He writes of huge wicker images packed with criminals which were burnt on the sacred festival days. According to his account the Celts worshipped the god of the underworld Dis and other deities he identified with Apollo, Mercury, Mars, Jupiter and Minerva. These were probably local Celtic gods and goddesses which were given Latin names as in the example of the horned god Cernnunos whose real Celtic name is unknown to us.

Pliny provides us with a graphic description of a druidic ritual of the cutting of the sacred mistletoe. This was a plant regarded by the Celts as a powerful healing agent. The ceremony took place on the sixth night of the waxing moon and included the sacrifice of two white bulls to the powers of Nature. A druid clad in a white robe (symbolizing the purity of spirit) climbs the tree and cuts a sprig of mistletoe with a golden sickle. The plant falls to the ground and is caught in a white cloak. The bulls are then led forward, their throats are cut with a ritual flint knife so that the blood soaks into the ground under the tree. Before this ritual the druids fasted and the mistletoe had to be cut only with the left (lunar) hand.

Pagans regarded the mistletoe as a very potent plant. It was regarded as an all-cure capable of healing any disease or illness. This claim has always been ridiculed up to now but recent experiments by a Swiss medical research team have provided evidence to support this. As we know, an arrow made of the mistletoe wood was used to kill the Norse god Baldur and in Sweden the plant is still regarded as sacred to the Thunder God Thor.

The mistletoe also has a sexual symbolism which is little known. In pagan times its white berries were regarded as symbolic of drops of semen. The oak tree, on which the plant sometimes grows as a parasite, was also regarded in ancient times as a phallic symbol. In fact the word *glans* for the conical head of the penis is derived from the Latin word for acorn. If you look at the shape of an acorn you will see why this is so. The innocent modern custom of kissing under the mistletoe is a very sublimated version of the old fertility rites once practised under the oak tree to ensure good harvests. It is for this reason that the mistletoe is the only winter greenery not allowed inside a church at Christmas time.

Indo-European Origins

Contrary to the distorted and biased accounts of their barbaric rites of human sacrifice by classical writers it seems certain that the Celtic druids were followers of the old Indo-European shamanistic tradition. Their ritual costume certainly suggests this is true. For instance the famous Irish druid MacRoth is said to have worn the skin of a dun-coloured bull and a speckled bird head dress. Although they may have used Stonehenge and other neolithic stone circles for major ceremonies the druids usually gathered in sacred groves known as *nemetons*. This is a typical shamanistic practice.

Novice druids had to undergo a training session lasting

up to twenty years and all the teachings were given orally in
the manner of the shamans. Like the shamans, the druids
were said to be able to fly, change shape into animals and
communicate with the birds. Their ceremonies included
ritual drumming, dancing and the use of the sacred
mushroom *amanita muscaria* or fly agaric. Either the druids
inherited shamanistic beliefs from their Indo-European
ancestors in Asia or they were taught them by the
aboriginal people they encountered when emigrating to
Western Europe.

What evidence is there that the druids knew of the runes
and their magical powers? In *Pugh's Welsh Dictionary* we find
a number of words with occult significance which are
derived from the old Celtic tongue. They are: *coel*, an omen
or superstition; *coel bren*, a piece of wood for casting lots; *coel
fain*, the stones of omen (runes?); and *coel y beirdd*, the
alphabet of the bards. According to the *New English
Dictionary coel* or *cole* is an old word meaning prophet,
magician or diviner.

The coel bren were also known as omen sticks and were
used by the chief druid to predict the future. They may be
similar or identical to the rods of yew engraved with ogham
sentences which were used by some druids for divination
purposes. These are described by the famous Celtic bard
Taliesin in a verse of one of his poems on magical themes.

I am Taliesin
Chief of the bards of the West.
I am acquainted with every sprig
in the cave of the arch diviner.

Druidic Tree Alphabet

A system of divination was also associated with the druidic
tree alphabet. This was known as the *Beth Luis Nion* from
the names of the three sacred trees of birch, rowan and ash.
In this alphabet the trees native to Britain were used by the
druids to symbolize letters of the ogham alphabet. They
also correspond to the letters of the Greek and Roman
alphabets as we can see below.

Roman	Celtic	Tree
A	Ailm	Silver Fir
B	Beth	Birch
C	Coll	Hazel
D	Duir	Oak
E	Eahda	Aspen
F	Fearn	Alder
G	Gort	Ivy
H	Uath	Hawthorn
I	Idho	Yew
L	Luis	Rowan
M	Muin	Vine
N	Nion	Ash
Ng	Ngetal	Reed
O	Ohn	Furze
R	Ruis	Elder
S	Saille	Willow
T	Tinne	Holly
U	Ura	Heather

The Celtics connected the thirteen original consonants of the ogham alphabet and their symbolic trees with the thirteen lunar months of the calendar used in pagan times. Each month had twenty-eight days in accordance with the phases of the moon. The yearly cycle began on November 1st, which was the Celtic New Year festival of Samhain or Summer End. The tree months are as follows.

Through the use of ogham (invented by the god Ogma, as the runes are credited to the god Odin) the bardic tree alphabet, the coel bren or omen sticks and the shamanistic practices, the druids are linked with the rune magicians of pagan Scandinavia.

A Vision of Oneness

We can now visualize a magical tradition based on the beliefs and rituals of the Old Religion of the shamans which was the root of the pagan spiritual philosophy of pre-Christian Europe. It was based on a reverence for Mother

Tree	Month	Deity	Esoteric Meaning
Birch	December 23 - January 20	Ceridwen	Beginning
Rowan	January 21 - February 17	Brigit	Magic
Ash	February 18 - March 17	Gwydion	Knowledge
Alder	March 18 - April 14	Bran	Strength
Willow	April 15 - May 12	Arianhod	Enchantment
Hawthorn	May 13 - June 9	Olwen	Fertility
Oak	June 10 - July 7	The Dagda	Power
Holly	July 8 - August 4	Cuchulain	Heroism
Hazel	August 5 - September 1	Mannanan	Wisdom
Bramble	September 2 - September 29	Sadv	Exaltation
Ivy	September 30 - October 27	Palu	Intoxication
Yew	October 28 - November 21	Gwyn	Death
Elder	November 22 - December 22	Cailleach	Rebirth

Earth, a belief in the omnipotent Life Force which permeated all living things in the universe and the acceptance of humanity's true role as the guardian of life on this green and beautiful planet of ours.

This book was written to present this pagan viewpoint to modern people searching for the mysteries of their past heritage. It reveals that this mystical tradition of the Oneness of all life is the true magical secret hidden within the druidic tree alphabet and the Norse runes.